PROLOGUE

Traveling through a continent known for its frequent earthquakes and volcanic eruptions, we should not have been surprised to encounter a landslide blocking our way. We were following an NBC film crew and their French driver, assuming they knew where they were going, as the road we were traveling was not shown on any map or GPS device, nor was it detailed on the Tripy guidance system installed in our truck by the Rally organizers. This was a shame because the road was quite pretty, winding along a river valley, cutting a deep gorge into cliffs colored in various hues of red and orange, merging into browns and beige. The sand, wind, and dust we had been fighting through the upper plateaus of Argentina had been replaced by lush groves of trees, bamboo, and the occasional market garden. The area also appeared to be a destination for adventure tourists, as a number of small inns and campgrounds lined the riverside, offering rock climbing and river rafting, with the local bars and restaurants crowded with young people in wet suits and colorful helmets carrying kayak paddles.

Abruptly, the road began to climb steeply away from the scenic river valley in a series of tight switchbacks as the smooth pavement petered away into what they call *ripio*, a mix of gravel, dirt, and rock, occasionally graded, but on this road not for some time. We were hoping we didn't meet someone coming down, as there was scarcely any room to pass, and the steep cliff plunging hundreds of feet straight down into the valley on the one side, with the rock wall close on the other, would cause severe heart attacks for both parties.

After crossing a massive hydroelectric dam, the road continued to climb, with its condition deteriorating even further. At the summit, a small hand-lettered sign was attached to a makeshift barrier stating that we should only proceed at our own risk. Being men, we ignored the warnings and continued on until we encountered the first pile of rubble strewn across the road. Clearly the slide of rock and sand from the cliffs along the road had been triggered by the 5.2 Richter scale earthquake that had shaken us awake earlier that morning. The pile of rubble was navigable by our two 4WD trucks, albeit very gingerly. At each turn in the makeshift road, however, we found yet another landslide, each becoming progressively wider and higher, and containing much larger boulders determined to ruin the underside of our vehicles.

After what turned out to be the final ascent and descent of a particularly nasty pile of fallen rocks, prudence demanded we take a look around the next corner, and it was a good thing we did. To our dismay, all we could see was the steep red cliff descending deeply into the river valley, with the single-lane road, once carved into its side, now covered with debris at least ten to twelve feet high extending as far as we could see into the distance. We were only a few kilometers from our destination, but the way forward was clearly impassable.

I slumped forward in defeat. It was so hot, I was so dirty, and I was so exhausted. What was I doing here? What were any of these people doing here?

ZERO TO SIXTY
A DAKAR ADVENTURE

Enjoy!

DAVID MILLS

Copyright © 2014 David G. Mills.

All rights reserved. No part of this book may be reproduced, stored, or transmitted by any means—whether auditory, graphic, mechanical, or electronic—without written permission of both publisher and author, except in the case of brief excerpts used in critical articles and reviews. Unauthorized reproduction of any part of this work is illegal and is punishable by law.

ISBN: 978-1-4834-0844-6 (sc)
ISBN: 978-1-4834-0843-9 (e)

Library of Congress Control Number: 2014902749

Because of the dynamic nature of the Internet, any web addresses or links contained in this book may have changed since publication and may no longer be valid. The views expressed in this work are solely those of the author and do not necessarily reflect the views of the publisher, and the publisher hereby disclaims any responsibility for them.

Certain images in this book are used with the permission of
Rodrigo Farias Moreno (www.fariasmoreno.com).

Lulu Publishing Services rev. date: 2/12/2014

CONTENTS

Prologue ix
Chapter One: Time to Fear 1
Chapter Two: Dealing with the "ASOs" 11
Chapter Three: Fireworks on New Year's Eve 25
Chapter Four: A Bivouac is a Very Noisy Place 37
Chapter Five: Preparing for a Dakar is Like Going to War 55
Chapter Six: The Perils of Driving in South America 67
Chapter Seven: Crossing the Andes: From +40°C to -5°C in One Day 79
Chapter Eight: Avoiding My "Bad Goofy" 91
Chapter Nine: Getting to Know Five Competitors 103
Chapter Ten: The Desert Dunes: The Real Dakar Begins ... 119
Chapter Eleven: Winning at Any Cost 129
Chapter Twelve: *Feche Feche*: The Bane of a Biker's Existence 137
Chapter Thirteen: A Most Disappointing Day 145
Chapter Fourteen: The Mysterious Nazca Lines 153
Chapter Fifteen: The 2012 Dakar Ends 161
Chapter Sixteen: What Does the Dakar Mean? 169
Acknowledgments 183

CHAPTER ONE
TIME TO FEAR

It's five o'clock in the morning on January 1, 2012, in Mar del Plata, Argentina. The temperature is already close to 30°C and climbing. Strong winds off the Atlantic Ocean are whipping up massive clouds of choking dust that permeated everything we ate and breathed. Normal people—if they are up at all this early on this particular day—are most likely still celebrating the arrival of the New Year or perhaps suffering the ill effects of revelries the night before. But here I am, fully dressed in my Tamarugal Honda Chile uniform, sober and alert, waiting at the start line for the initial Stage of the 2012 Dakar Rally.

We have been sequestered for the last three days inside a heavily guarded naval base, home to the main force of the Argentinian Navy. I am standing where this navy set sail to tangle with the British over the Falkland Islands—or the Malvinas, as the Argentinians call them—some thirty years ago. Almost 650 Argentinian soldiers and sailors perished in the conflict, including the 323 drowned with the sinking of the *General Belgrano* by the British submarine HMS *Conqueror*. Beside me, tied up along the docks, rising and falling slowly and languidly with the ocean tides, are some of those same ships, massive destroyers, corvettes, and battleships, all bristling with guns, cannons, and I don't know what other instruments of destruction. It is a surreal atmosphere as the sailors look down on us as we get ready to leave their home.

I cautiously inspect my immediate surroundings to ensure I am not near any British competitors; there may be some lingering animosity from the loss of that infamous war.

Lined up in pairs behind me are 185 high-powered, custom-designed off-road motorcycles; 33 quad ATVs; 171 specialized four-wheel-drive vehicles; and 76 large trucks, their riders, drivers, and copilots anxiously waiting to determine if they have the stuff to win, or simply finish, what is the world's most prestigious, arduous, and dangerous off-road race.

The Dakar, once more famously known as the Paris Dakar Rally, was created by French motorcycle racer Thierry Sabine, who became lost during a 1977 race in the Libyan Desert. Believing others, like him, would want to challenge their endurance, strength, and persistence in driving across uncharted terrain, he set out from Paris the next year with 180 other teams to see who could travel the fastest to the northern African city of Dakar, Senegal.

The Dakar exists in an automotive racing class called Rally Raid, which can run as few as three days or as long as fourteen. There are a number of well-known Rally Raids, including the Rallye des Pharaohs in the Middle East, the Silk Way Rally through the steppes of Russia, the Baja in Mexico, the Targa in Canada's Newfoundland, and the Mint 400, made infamous in Hunter S. Thompson's pharmaceutically inspired book, *Fear and Loathing in Las Vegas.*

The Dakar is the world's premier Rally Raid. It is the largest, the longest, the most difficult, and the main prize for anyone competing in the Rally world. It is the Holy Grail of Rally, and has been held every year but one since 1978. During preparations for the 2008 edition, four French Dakar enthusiasts were murdered in Mauritania, allegedly by al-Qaeda insurgents. The terrorist group then claimed it would use Dakar competitors crossing the African desert as target practice. The organizers reluctantly, but wisely, canceled the race on the eve of its departure, and the following year, searching for a region with similar terrain and natural challenges but with a safer and more stable political environment, moved the Dakar to South America. It has been there ever since.

Professional racers sponsored by the world's leading corporations vie for the glory of winning the event, supported by huge teams of mechanics, doctors, massage therapists, sports psychologists, and chefs, with massive inventories of spare vehicles and parts. More famous participants include Formula 1 drivers Jacky Ickx and Eliseo Salazar, NASCAR superstar Robby Gordon, movie star Charley Boorman, and British Prime Minister Margaret Thatcher's son, Mark, who became lost in the Sahara desert for four days during his Dakar. But the majority of competitors are called "privateers," people who risk enormous amounts of their own money—as well as their health and well-being—simply to see if they can finish the world's most difficult and challenging automotive competition.

The Dakar is truly one of the toughest challenges man and machine can face. Racing against the clock across dirt and gravel roads, unmarked track, grasslands, mountain valleys, and shifting desert sand dunes, competitors run the Dakar for fourteen days in early January each year. As a testament to the dangers encountered throughout the race, more than fifty people have been killed since the Dakar's founding in 1978.

This year, competitors will travel a total of 8,400 kilometers, of which 4,400 kilometers were timed to determine the winners of the fourteen days of racing. They will drive through three countries: Argentina, Chile, and, for the first time, Peru, the twenty-seventh country visited by the Dakar. A total of 465 vehicles are departing today, along with their numerous support vehicles and crews. Competitors will represent more than fifty nations, with just over 30 percent entering their first Dakar Rally. An estimated five million spectators will experience the Rally along its route, with an expected television and online audience of over ninety million closely following its progress. The Dakar is truly one of the premiere automotive and sporting events of the year.

As I stand in the hot New Year's Day sun, waiting for the racers to leave, for the gazillionth time I think about how many people have died during the Dakar. I ponder the dangers I will face around every corner, every day, for the next two weeks. I remember the countless medical forms and waivers we signed over the previous three days in which doctors warned us about the threats of malaria, yellow and dengue fever, rabies, cholera, hepatitis, E. coli, salmonella, the hantavirus pulmonary syndrome, and many other afflictions, including the real possibility of dehydration and altitude sickness.

I had heard about dengue fever. Apparently, a mild case can seem like a simple flu bug, but each year more than half a million people become seriously ill from the disease, experiencing hemorrhagic fevers that cause vomiting and often bleeding from the nose, mouth, and skin.

Pain can be so acute, the disease is often called "breakbone fever." Are you kidding? Pain so bad you break a bone from writhing in agony?

And then there is Chagas disease, a wasting fever and ultimately heart failure caused by a small beetle that burrows under your skin and then propagates, sending its tiny little eggs into your bloodstream, where they hatch in and around your heart, killing you slowly as you succumb to the disease, weighing a pittance of what you used to, unable to absorb nutrients, with your heart failing in the final stages. My son had contracted the disease while sand surfing in Peru the year before, luckily finding a doctor who tested him for the disease when he was quite ill. Apparently, if you don't catch it at an early stage, you are toast.

I started to agonize all over again. *What the hell am I doing here?* I cast my eyes quickly away from the bristling gunships and onto the ground around me, looking to see if any small bugs were scurrying toward my bare legs, teeth bared, seeking a home for their young.

My Dakar adventure began in 2005, when my wife and I purchased and renovated an abandoned stone castle overlooking the Maipo River southeast of Santiago, Chile, in the foothills of the Andes Mountains. Following the two-plus years it took to actually own and then rejuvenate the property, I embarked on a brief sabbatical by motorcycle to learn more about our adopted country. I have owned motorcycles most of my adult life and toured throughout the world, but Chile is among the most perfectly suited countries for motorcycling. The roads are in excellent condition, they provide lots of challenging terrain, and between the months of November and April it is always hot and never rains. Rain and motorcycling are not a pleasant combination.

In January 2008, the Dakar made its first appearance in central Chile, holding its traditional mid-Rally rest day in the city of Valparaiso on the Pacific coast, about two hours from our home. I had heard about the Rally and rode to Valparaiso to see what all the fuss was about. It was quite a sight. The bivouac in Valparaiso was huge, with hundreds of people working feverishly to repair and rejuvenate their vehicles for the last half of the competition. Thousands and thousands of fans surrounded the heavily guarded fences delineating the bivouac, all trying to get a glimpse of their favorite Rally stars, including a number of local Chilean heroes. The country's president made an official visit, as did large groups of sponsor VIPs, basking in the glory of actually being inside the bivouac. I was intrigued by the sheer size of the event, the frantic activity within the bivouac, and the huge number of knowledgeable enthusiasts I overheard outside the fences discussing various aspects of the Rally so far and what they were seeing going on inside.

The next year, I took my motorcycle and traveled into Chile's northern regions to meet the Dakar as it moved south from La Serena toward Santiago before crossing back into Argentina and the final days of competition racing to Buenos Aires. The Rally had covered most of Chile's northern deserts, already taking a significant toll on the competitors: of the 407 vehicles that started the race a week earlier, only 203 remained to try and finish. As I followed the Rally for its final three days in Chile, it was fascinating to experience both the racing and, watching from outside the fence, life in the bivouacs, where the racers and their crews live for the duration of the Rally. I was hooked.

On returning to our Chilean home, I was excited about trying to get a closer look at the Rally, its people, and the Dakar adventure. My wife had always supported my periodic adventures, so I was confident she would have no objections. Then again, I had not told her about the fifty people who had been killed during the event's history!

One evening, shortly after my return, we had a group of friends to our home for dinner. Sitting under the massive fig tree that dominates our garden, Ghilson, a handsome Brazilian man and a companion of our neighbor, apologized that he had to take a call on his cell phone. We did not know this gentleman—in Chile invited guests often turn up unexpectedly, bringing a number of their friends. It can make for a chaotic evening, but it also can result in a lot of interesting newfound relationships.

After a long conversation on his phone, Ghilson told us that unfortunately he had to leave. We discovered that he was a renowned South American sports psychologist who counted among his clients Chaleco Lopez, the top Chilean motorcyclist competing in that year's Dakar. Chaleco had crashed and suffered a very bad fall on the second-to-last day of the event. He had been forced to retire from the race, and Ghilson was flying to Buenos Aires that evening to meet with him.

I was stunned. Here was a dinner guest, uninvited or not, who could potentially provide me with an entrance into the exclusive and protected world of the Dakar.

"Do you think I could meet Chaleco?" I asked hopefully. "I really want to learn more about the Dakar."

"Sure," he answered. "Let's see how he is when he gets back to Santiago."

I was beaming. And then Ximena, one of our constant good friends in Chile, spoke up.

"I know someone else who is in the Dakar. A friend of mine works for an executive whose son is competing this year. The son's name is Daniel Gouët."

Daniel is an accomplished motocross and enduro rider, and he had entered his first Dakar this year at the age of twenty-four. He had started the race in 148th position in the motorcycle category and ultimately finished a remarkable 25th. Just to finish a Dakar is a significant accomplishment, especially on your first try, but moving up into the elite rankings so quickly garnered him a lot of attention and acclaim.

"Do you think you could set something up? I'd love to meet Daniel too," I said.

"Most certainly. I'll call her tomorrow."

Within two days my wife and I were sitting in the bar at the luxurious new W Hotel in downtown Santiago with Daniel and his father, Pedro. It had been only three weeks since Daniel's triumphant return from his strong placing in the Dakar. I related my newfound fascination with the Rally and wondered if I could join their team for next year's event in whatever capacity they desired. I also explained that I wanted to write a book about my experiences, the Rally, its history, and the people who risk everything to compete.

As I described my ambitions, I noticed that my wife was much more interested in Daniel's colorful and copious tattoos peeking below the arms of his shirtsleeves. Our eldest son's upper torso is also covered with body art, and she knew that all the markings meant something. As Pedro and I carried on our conversation in broken English, Karen and Daniel chatted away in much more broken Spanish. Their chat suddenly evolved into a display that the well-dressed businesspeople in the bar likely will never witness again. When asked about his designs,

Daniel, a fit and handsome young man, obliged my wife by standing up and whipping off his T-shirt to explain what his tattoos meant. To my mind, her education seemed to take a lot longer than it should have, with Karen paying rapt attention to his bare chest and muscled arms, especially as Daniel spoke a very rapid Chilean Spanish, and I suspect that Karen probably only understood about 10 percent of what he said.

As this tableau was unfolding beside us in one of Santiago's most chic venues, Pedro and I continued our discussions about the potential of my joining the team. After a few minutes, Pedro got on his phone and invited Sergio Baracatt, the head of Honda Chile and a major sponsor of the team, to join us. Daniel rode for Honda, and Sergio had been a big promoter of Daniel's career.

Once Sergio arrived, I repeated my story, asking to come along for the ride. They were all clearly perplexed as to why a Canadian businessman nearing his sixtieth birthday would want to endure the punishment, dangers, and sleep deprivation of a Dakar Rally. And why would a gringo with a faltering grasp of the Spanish language want to join a Chilean team? There were so many obstacles, so many problems, so many difficulties inherent in my attempting to make it through the fourteen days of the Dakar. But Chileans believe the best in people; they are trusting and are always open to new ideas. Despite their reservations, to my surprise and delight, they agreed to allow me to come, and I was welcomed into the Tamarugal Honda Racing XC Rally team for the next edition of the Dakar Rally.

As we drove home from the meeting, the grin on my face slowly transitioned into lines of worry. What was I getting myself into? Our lives in Chile had become very comfortable, and with a busy career in Canada, our visits to South America were supposed to be a chance for rest, relaxation, some luxury travel, and generally a time to wind down. I had endured a number of adventures in my younger days—kayaking, hiking, and canoeing in Canada's Arctic and other wilderness locations; long bicycle trips; and many motorcycle tours in North America, Europe, and our newly adopted home in Chile. But nothing would prepare me for what I might encounter on the Dakar. And I certainly was not getting any younger, my fitness level left much to be desired, and, to be honest, now that a dream was becoming a reality, I confessed that I might not be up to the challenge. I was having second thoughts already. It slowly was dawning on me that this would be an adventure of epic proportions.

Now, almost a year later, here I was at the start line for the inception of the 2012 Dakar, with those same million questions and insecurities racing through my head. Would I make it through the entire race—more than 8,400 kilometers in only fourteen days? What about the language barrier? Everyone on the team spoke only Spanish, and my lack of fluency could be a big problem, perhaps even a danger to me and those around me. I could clearly envision someone waving and yelling frantically to me in a language I could not understand, not realizing that I was about to be slammed into by an unseen out-of-control racing car or crushed by some large piece of equipment. I was getting really scared.

There was also the issue known as the "observer effect," often called the "Heisenberg principle," referring to changes that the act of observation can make on the activities being observed. Would I experience the *real* Dakar or a sanitized version presented to me as an outsider? I did not want to be that guy, the punter, who was only along for the ride. Adding to my apprehension was the fact that I am truly no mechanic. If I even pick up a screwdriver, I immediately begin to bleed and, thus, could not really help the team and its efforts. The ultimate testament to my ineptness with tools is caught on a short Christmas home movie showing my three-year-old son holding a plastic hammer up to the camera and saying, "Look, Dad, I got an 'oh shit' as a present." *Oh, dear.*

Ultimately, I was worried I would only be in the way, stumbling around in the dark, causing problems as I tried to chronicle the team's challenges and adventures, interfering in necessary work with dumb questions. Would the team accept me or ignore me as some kind of wannabe tagging along? I remembered the tale from a friend who had encountered a charging rhinoceros during a safari in Africa, one of the most dangerous animals on our planet. As the enraged, huge behemoth bore down on their safari vehicle, their guide crouched down in the back corner of the truck, covered his head, and said, "Time to fear."

I was terrified. It was my time to fear.

CHAPTER TWO
DEALING WITH THE ASOS

Three days before the start of the race, we had arrived in Mar del Plata, Argentina, the oceanside city where the 2012 Dakar would begin. We had spent two very long days transporting the team and its vehicles from Santiago, Chile, crossing the Andes Mountains and the interminably flat, featureless, and boring pampas of central Argentina.

My driving companion was Rodrigo Farias, the team's photographer and press liaison. Pedro Gouët, Daniel's father, would be joining us later for most of the trip.

Rodrigo is a handsome and fit young man with sharp blue eyes sparkling above his dark mustache and jet-black curly hair. Thirty years of age, he had just experienced the birth of his first child, Leon, only four weeks before leaving Santiago. Leon would become a constant topic of conversation and an invisible partner through much of the Rally.

In his day job, Rodrigo owns a successful business making documentary films about surfing in Chile. His partner, Ramon Navarro, is one of the country's top surfers and well-known in the sport around the world. Before leaving on the Dakar, Rodrigo had been working on a film detailing the genesis of surfing in Chile in the early 1960s. During his research he met many of the country's surf pioneers and gathered all of their old home movies documenting the beginnings of the sport both before and after the repressive Pinochet coup of September 11, 1973. It will be a wonderful and fascinating documentary.

But now he is entering the world of high-performance motor sports and will be applying his skill as a sports photographer to document the Tamarugal team through all fourteen days of the competition, relaying his photos, videos, and commentary to the Chilean and international press for the entire 2012 Dakar. Most importantly for me, Rodrigo is fluent in English and would prove invaluable as I navigated the Dakar world and the Tamarugal team over the next two weeks.

The 400-kilometer drive south from Buenos Aires to Mar del Plata provided the first glimpse of what we would be experiencing on the Dakar. All of the race and support vehicles from Europe—and there are a lot of Europeans in the Dakar—had arrived by boat in Buenos Aires, where they had been off-loaded and driven to Mar del Plata. It is a technical and logistical magic act to get all of the Dakar entourage—the race and support vehicles, medical teams and supplies, the organizers, and everything and everyone else—from points around the world to arrive in time to be registered and start the Dakar on January 1. Thus, on our way south we saw and met a number of teams with their race and support vehicles and crews. It was sinking in that my Dakar was really going to happen.

We also noticed that there were a lot of police in Argentina. About every five kilometers we would see a set of yellow flags with a couple of officers and their vehicles, watching the cars go by. I am not sure what purpose they were serving. There did not appear to be any radar detecting speeds, nor did they seem to want to pull anyone over to check papers, as they do in Chile. They were just there, some sleeping, some reading, many having a snack, with most just sitting around chatting. One officer did stop us, but only to ask if we would drive him to the next town. We saw another hitchhiking. Rodrigo and I surmised that with so many people on the police force, they must not pay them very much.

We arrived at our hotel in Mar del Plata late in the evening, finding much of the team already there. The race cars and motorcycles, as well as the two large transport trucks carrying all of our parts and supplies, were parked below us in the Rally's opening bivouac. The hotel and the opening bivouac would be our home for the next three days of registration.

Mar del Plata is Argentina's answer to France's Riviera, Brazil's Rio de Janeiro, or Italy's Amalfi Coast. Situated on the Atlantic Ocean about four hundred kilometers south of Buenos Aires, the city was founded in 1874 as a sort of European bathing resort where the wealthy elite from Buenos Aires could travel south by train to enjoy the ocean and relax in the city's spas and hotels. During the 1940s and 1950s, the character of the city and its visitors changed dramatically as Juan Perón's socialist government constructed a large number of cheap hotels and guesthouses, allowing more middle class and the working poor to visit the city, a tradition that continues today. Many of the pre-Perón French- and Italian-style villas and mansions still remain, most carefully preserved as museums. The beaches are crowded, many being private, and the nightlife is busy, robust, and active until the early morning hours.

With a permanent population of some six hundred thousand, it is the country's seventh largest city. However, during the peak summer months and holiday season of January and February, tourism can swell the populace to well over two million, with an estimated eight million visitors coming to the city annually. But this holiday season, adding to the tens of thousands of revelers already in the city to celebrate the arrival of the New Year were more than three thousand competitors, support teams, and organizing staff necessary to register, document, coordinate, and check credentials for the beginning of the 2012 Dakar.

To become an official participant in the Dakar, you need to pass a lot of tests. The rigor is partly because the organizers are from France, and the French can be a tad bureaucratic, but mostly it is to ensure the safety and well-being of everyone involved and to force a level playing field for all participants.

The Dakar is owned and managed by France's Amaury Sport Organisation (ASO), the same people who bring bicycling's premier event, the Tour de France, to the world, in addition to some forty other sporting fixtures, including other well-known cycling races as the Paris-Roubaix and the Tour of Oman, the Paris Marathon for runners, and golf's Alstom Open and the Lacoste Ladies Open.

When I first heard of the organization, it was referred to as "Los ASOs." South Americans generally do not pronounce an acronym by each letter but rather as a whole word. For example, the YMCA near our home in Chile is pronounced as *"el imca."* You can then understand why, when my Chilean friends talked about *"los asos,"* it brought a smile to my face. I knew the French could be a bit arrogant at times, but calling them *"asos"* seemed a little extreme. But as I proceeded through the three days of registration, I found myself occasionally muttering, "What an *aso*," under my breath.

Our hotel was situated on a steep hill running down to the ocean and the location of the opening bivouac, a sequestered area occupying most of the naval base on the south side of the city. On our first morning, after a good sleep and a team breakfast, we all strolled down the hill and through the tight security at the bivouac's entrance.

It was an amazing sight. The naval base occupied about ten acres extending along a point of land jutting into the ocean beside one of the most popular beaches in the city. As I walked along the seawall under the hot sun, at times enjoying the view of the bikini-clad sunbathers on the shoreline beside me, I was surrounded by the race—cars, motorcycles quads, and trucks—with mechanics crawling all over to get them ready. Surrounding me were hundreds of competition and support vehicles undergoing last-minute preparations to ensure they would pass the coming days' rigorous inspections, while drivers and crew made sure all their credentials were checked.

The vehicles, brightly colored and covered with sponsor logos, appeared like raptors, mean-looking, technological wonders, with speed and endurance written all over them. The team personnel all wore uniforms, again plastered with logos and the flags of their home countries. Tents were set up, awnings provided shade from the hot sun, and the huge transport trucks holding all the necessary tools and equipment loomed over the race vehicles to form private team compounds. A myriad of languages were being shouted above the noise of high-performance engines being warmed up, tested, and checked, getting ready for the two weeks of intense and dangerous competition ahead.

It was chaos, but at the same time there was a sense of order in the heat, the swirling dust, and the humidity. Everyone seemed to have a mission, a task, a goal, and a job to do. Trucks, cars, and motorcycles swarmed up and down the roads between the team compounds, people sitting on the roofs, dangling from the sides and back, all heading to and fro, gathering parts and papers, or to queue for the beginning of the registration process. It was hot, it was dirty, and it was my first taste of how crazy my life with the Dakar would be.

ZERO TO SIXTY

Our first task was to obtain our Dakar accreditation, and to start the process we visited the press area just outside the fenced-in and heavily guarded main bivouac. It was my first taste of not only the bureaucracy necessary to organize the Dakar, but also the legions of fans that would become a part of my everyday experience over the ensuing two weeks. Surrounding the bivouac were thousands of people, some residents of Mar del Plata, but many others who had traveled to South America specifically to experience the Dakar, all of them zeroing in on someone like me, wearing a team uniform.

"Hey, gringo, over here. Can I have your autograph? Can I take your picture with my wife? With my kids? Do you have any stickers, caps, or T-shirts I can have?" The calls and requests were constant, coming from all directions as I worked my way through the crowds to get to the press trailer. I now understood why the ASO had hired more than twenty-five thousand police and military along the route to control the crowds.

I was classified as "*Prensa—Escritor*" (Press—Writer) with credentials in an "assistance vehicle." It costs much less to participate as "press," and by agreeing not to enter the racecourse with our truck, it did not have to be adapted with roll bars, special lights, and a host of other expensive safety features and equipment.

The press center was a small trailer just outside the huge main registration tents. A line was already forming with everyone clustered near the door, both trying to bully their way to the front and also to find some shade from the increasingly intense heat from the rising sun. Thida Sengounthone, a beautiful young Frenchwoman of Malaysian descent, was in charge of press accreditation for the ASO, and she must have possessed the patience of Job to deal with the crowds and cramped quarters with which she was forced to work. Thida became my guiding light through the registration process, a helpful presence as we worked our way through the complicated process of becoming official Dakar participants.

In addition to various media guides, participant lists and profiles, route maps, a cute little data key shaped like a Volkswagen Amarok truck (a major sponsor for this year's Dakar), containing reams of information about the Rally, we were given our encoded press badges containing our photo. We were told that these badges must be worn at all times, and she was not kidding—they were checked many times each day to ensure we were legitimate. We were also presented with a cream-colored "passport" with pages of checkpoints we needed to have stamped to make sure everyone had the right information. After more than five hours of standing around in the hot sun, waiting and then meeting with Thida, we finally walked into the huge registration tents nearby, clutching our passports and waving our badges at the security forces, to begin the registration process.

The first and most important credential check was to ensure all appropriate fees had been paid. It's not inexpensive to enter the Dakar Rally. The fee for a motorcycle was thirteen thousand pounds, while the cars were charged twenty-two thousand pounds. My fee to enter as a member of the press was a more modest three thousand pounds.

This first checkpoint immediately became an issue for us. While everyone else on the team had been registered with their various fees paid and tied to their names, Rodrigo and I were somehow not on the list. Our team manager could show that the amounts owing for us had been remitted, but the ASO had somehow not attributed the payments to our registered names. It took hours to get this problem straightened out, primarily because the *aso* from the ASO kept walking away from us to talk to his buddies and then disappearing behind a busy desk to handle other issues, waving his finger at me in that annoying way only the French can do when I tried to attract his attention. Finally, they reluctantly acknowledged that we had paid, that we were registered, and with everything properly tied together, that we were good to go.

The remainder of the registration went quite smoothly. We would approach a desk where a friendly and helpful official would guide us through what we had to do. We provided phone numbers, passport numbers, driver's licenses, vehicle ownerships and other papers, proof of insurance, contact information for next of kin to notify should something happen, customs declarations for crossing the border, medical forms, gasoline forms, and a host of other checks. There were also innumerable waivers to be signed, absolving everyone and anyone from the responsibility for anything that could happen to us on the Dakar. As I signed these waivers, again and again, I began to question anew what I had got myself into.

ZERO TO SIXTY

The most complicated checkpoint was the desk where we obtained our registered Tripy system. The Tripy is a proprietary GPS device that had to be hardwired into our vehicle and encoded with our truck's number and the names of everyone in it. The Tripy provides detailed directions for the entire route of the 2012 Dakar, including the location of all the bivouacs. It is like a preprogrammed GPS system, without the annoying Esperanto voice telling you where to turn or that you have gone the wrong way ("Recalculating!"). Instead, the route is shown as a progressive line with directions you must follow, including all turns, routes, and towns marked as you approach them.

The Tripy also monitors your speed. If you exceed any posted speed limit—and the Tripy knows them all, in every town and on every highway—it beeps at you loudly and persistently, beginning with a series of blips as you approach the speed limit, and then a much louder, penetrating, and constant scream if you go over the limit. Your team can be penalized if you consistently exceed posted limits. We would become very adept at using our truck's cruise control to avoid the Tripy's annoying warnings.

The lineups for most of the registration stations were long, but the entire system was very well organized. With almost three thousand people needing to pass all the inspections, it was a very busy place. Surprisingly, I saw little sign of tempers flaring, which is something considering the many different languages being spoken, the heat, the lines, the fact that the French were organizing the event, and almost everyone waiting for clearance was a man with a massive ego.

Once you passed your personal checks, you then took your vehicle for labeling and inspection. After installing our Tripy into our truck, we drove into the massive tents assigned to check all vehicles participating in the Dakar. There were four lanes, three of which were designated for competition and other vehicles that wanted to drive on the actual race routes, with the fourth reserved for support vehicles like ours that did not require the safety gear necessary to drive off-road.

As we entered the tent, we immediately faced a new obstacle. Somehow our truck had been assigned two different numbers, a situation that caused a significant problem when we attempted to get all the stickers identifying our vehicle as approved for the Dakar Rally and allowing us to enter the bivouacs each day. There was a lot of confusion at the credentials desk, especially as the inspection folks also had us listed as needing access to the racecourse, and clearly our truck did not have any of the necessary equipment. After a tense hour of waiting and negotiation, the officials finally issued our truck with an entirely new number, the third of the day. We parked to the side, and I had to run back into the credentials trailer to ensure all the stations we had visited were updated with our new truck number.

As I was waiting for the new truck number to be assigned, I wandered around the rest of the inspection area, watching as the actual race vehicles were examined. Each underwent a rigorous set of checks to ensure they had all the necessary safety equipment, but also to confirm each met the appropriate specifications for their respective race category. These inspections, known as "homogulation" in Rally terms, are designed by the Fédération Internationale de l'Automobile (FIA), the world's governing body for all motorsports. Interestingly, the term GTO following an automotive brand name refers to *Gran Turismo Omologato*, or homogulated, meaning "approved for racing." The regulations and specifications for the Dakar are contained in thick manuals that outline the myriad of details for engine size and displacement, horsepower, ventilation, aspiration, exhaust, suspension, and everything that could possibly give one vehicle an advantage over another. While safety is of paramount importance, the ASO also strives to give everyone a level playing field, placing the emphasis for winning on driving and navigation skills rather than technology.

Five or six ASO-uniformed technicians clutching the appropriate specification manual crawled over each vehicle, peering into everything and asking detailed questions about topics so esoteric I sometimes wondered what language they were speaking. I know a little about cars and motorcycles, but the depth and sophistication of these vehicles, and the length to which the inspectors would go to make sure everything conformed, was astonishing. It also took a very long time—three long days to get all 465 race and support vehicles passed.

While our inspection was not as rigorous as an "assistance vehicle," we still had to have certain specified safety equipment, a spare tire, towing devices, and a fire extinguisher, among other things. The inspectors also made sure we had the ominous-sounding seat-belt cutter and window-smashing hammer for each passenger, as well as our names and blood types clearly marked near each window. Why did they need my blood type posted on the vehicle? I pictured myself suspended in the truck cab, upside down in a river, trying to cut and smash my way to freedom, with only the comfort of knowing that if I was badly injured, at least they would know what type of blood to give me as a transfusion, and if I did not make it, they would know whom to call. I quickly convinced myself that I really should not be having these thoughts.

Once the inspections were completed, we moved to the labeling part of the tent where our number, along with Dakar-branded stickers and large labels, was affixed to our truck. We had to be readily recognized as a Dakar-approved vehicle from the air and all sides on the ground, while the special RFID device installed on our windshield would be read by security along the course and at all bivouacs. When the labeling team was finished, our truck, not only covered with Honda Racing logos and colors, now had Dakar insignia all over it.

Rodrigo and I hopped into the cab, looked at each other with big grins on our faces, and proudly drove out the other side of the tent. We were now an official Dakar participant with the ID number "1088" on the roof, sides, back, and front of our truck. I had to admit it looked pretty cool. The truck would be noticed immediately wherever we drove, and once again the sense of where I was and what I was about to do overwhelmed me. But there was no turning back now.

As our newly approved vehicle exited the inspection area, we found ourselves "backstage" at the official reception. An estimated crowd of some 120,000 fans had paid to watch as each race vehicle was driven onto a stage, and the drivers were interviewed beside a dozen or so gorgeous and scantily clad young women lining the stage, holding umbrellas. On leaving the stage, the bikes, quads, cars, and trucks were then sequestered in the *Parque Ferme* (Closed Parking Area) where they could not be touched until the race started on New Year's Day. It was amazing to experience the noise and excitement as each driver took the stage, with the loudest cheers reserved for the South American participants.

With the tough job of getting everything approved behind us, I returned to the Dakar bivouac to supposedly meet the rest of the team at the Chile tourism center within the public area. Being a good gringo, I arrived on time along with the three US-based car mechanics, also good gringos who turn up when they are told.

As we stood around in our team uniforms, waiting for the others, a few families stopped and asked if they could have their pictures taken with us. Then more people came, attracted by the cluster of initial fans, and then more and more, until suddenly we had over one hundred people crowding around us to see what was happening and to have their pictures taken with us, thinking we must somehow be important, or why else would all these people want our picture? It was all very odd, and after our twenty minutes of fame, we agreed to disperse in different directions. I now understand why celebrities avoid the paparazzi.

Following my brief time as a star, I attended the compulsory briefing for press cars. The main messages concerned speeding and obeying all traffic laws. During the previous year's Dakar, the organizers had received numerous complaints about vehicles driving too fast, running stoplights, and a host of other infractions. We saw pictures taken by spectators of huge assistance trucks passing long lines of vehicles on blind curves, another driving at a small car that was forced into a ditch, and others clearly running red lights. This year the organization was cracking down, and, in addition to monitoring our speeds through the Tripy system, there would be severe financial or time penalties for your team if infractions were serious or continued after warnings. Imagine what would happen if a competitor lost a podium finish because a stupid press car continually drove over the speed limit. I vowed we would listen to our cruise control and Tripy system and obey all laws, something I was not accustomed to doing in my normal motorcycle riding existence.

During the afternoon, the excitement started to build. The podium celebrations, the official introduction of the racers to the world, were being held in Mar del Plata's Plaza San Martin, a four-block square in the center of the city. With my press pass, I could go anywhere I pleased, and I spent the first few hours strolling inside the crowd barriers, watching the fans interact with the competitors. It was a hot, sunny day, the heat tempered by a fresh ocean breeze off the nearby Atlantic. Bleachers had been set up to hold the crowds, and the old stone buildings surrounding the square had fans hanging from every window, roof, and doorway. To keep everyone entertained, there were exhibitions of trick motorcycle driving, music, and tons of pretty girls from sponsoring organizations throwing free samples of energy drinks, energy bars, newspapers, coupons for telecommunications services, and other items into the crowd. And don't forget it was the afternoon of New Year's Eve, and everyone was seriously getting into a party mood.

The opening celebrations began with a group photograph on the steps of the main city hall. All 480 racers came together in a mass of humanity, all grinning exuberantly in their riding suits and protective clothing, carrying their helmets. If there was any apprehension about what they faced, it was lost in the anticipation of beginning the Dakar the next day. You could see on their faces the knowledge that the months and sometimes years of preparation would face the ultimate test beginning tomorrow. It was also sobering for me to stand in front of the large group, knowing there was a good chance many of them would not reach the finish, and possibly some would be badly injured or lose their lives.

Following the convocation photo, we all filed into a huge auditorium on the square for the first of what would become the daily drivers' briefings. As we entered the room, we were each given a headset and receiver so that we would be able to listen to translators providing the presentations in any number of different languages. The room was packed to the rafters, and sitting with the rest of the Tamarugal team, we listened intently as we learned details about the next day's route and were once again cautioned by the head of the Argentinian Police about obeying all traffic laws. Fuel details were reviewed, customs regulations were provided, and a host of other information was relayed. Clearly the Dakar Rally was becoming very real for everyone, and when the youngest competitor in this year's edition, a twenty-year-old Argentinian motorcyclist, read out the Dakar Charter, under which every competitor must live, there was complete silence. It was a very poignant moment after a few days of fun in the sun. Then everyone left to board buses and return to the *Parque Ferme*, where the competitors would collect their vehicles and prepare for the introductions at the podium celebrations.

As the briefing was taking place, the crowds outside had grown in number, and with the music and the noise of high-powered engines, it soon became a deafening roar. The *Parque Ferme* was about five kilometers from the podium, and authorities had closed the multilane seaside highway to accommodate the racers and their vehicles moving to and from the podium. Crowds, estimated at some five hundred thousand, lined the entire route to watch the competitors drive by. As I walked around the streets leading to the square where the podium was located, I could catch snatches of media interviews with the racers as they calculated their chances of winning, who was being touted as most likely to finish first, and if they were proud to represent their country, all making sure their sponsors' names and logos were prominently mentioned and displayed for the photographers.

On reaching the podium, each participant would drive up a ramp where they were introduced and interviewed for the crowds of fans and the numerous global television networks covering the event. Then each drove down into a holding area where accredited press could take their picture and talk to them, after which they returned to the *Parque Ferme* to await the 5:00 a.m. departure the next day.

Many used the podium celebration to showcase their driving skills. A perennial favorite, US NASCAR driver Robby Gordon stole the show. After his podium interview, he circled back behind the ramp and sped up and over, pushing his bright-orange Hummer high into the air. On landing, he performed a number of high-speed spins in front of the cheering crowd, with all four tires smoking and the engine roaring. If this was a sample of his driving on the actual racecourse, the fans were in for two highly entertaining weeks of competition.

As the celebrations continued through the day, I took the opportunity to walk back along the route toward the bivouac. Crowds of fans lined the almost five kilometers of highway, sitting in lawn chairs or on blankets with food and wine, watching the procession. Every competitor was accorded a welcome and a round of cheering as they went by, demonstrating the appreciation Mar del Plata felt for the Dakar choosing their city to launch the 2012 edition. After a while, I left the crowds and walked up a side street, away from the celebrations, catching a taxi back to our hotel. Tonight was New Year's Eve, we would be getting together with the entire team for a final celebratory dinner, and tomorrow would be a very early start.

CHAPTER THREE
FIREWORKS ON NEW YEAR'S EVE

The team's New Year's Eve celebration was a muted affair. After all, with the Dakar officially beginning at 5:00 a.m. the next morning, and everyone having to get ready to leave hours before the start time, it would have been irresponsible for anyone to misbehave. Still, we did have a small team dinner, hosted by Don Omar Campillay.

Don Omar is the main sponsor of the Tamarugal Honda Racing team, and he is the owner of Transportes Tamarugal Ltda, one of Chile's largest transportation and logistics companies. He is a powerfully built man, tanned, with a big smile, sharp penetrating eyes, and a soft voice. He clearly demands respect, and most of the people who work for his company have been with him for many years. He is a tough and successful businessman, but it is obvious he cares for his employees, including them in his large and extended family who visited us numerous times in bivouacs along the route.

Legend has it that Don Omar began his business in the 1960s with forty mules working in partnership with a mine owner in northern Chile, hauling ore and supplies to and from the mining property. Today, his business empire spans numerous activities, including vineyards, grape exports, trucking, and logistics. As the Dakar convoy moved through northern Chile, we passed many large trucks on the highways bearing the distinctive Tamarugal yellow, all honking their air horns to greet us.

A self-made man, he is very proud of his accomplishments, and so he should be. But Don Omar's greatest passion is Rally Raid, and as one of Chile's first Rally competitors, he distinguished himself in the early days of the sport in South America. Now his son, Javier, is following in his father's footsteps and is a key member of the 2012 Tamarugal team, driving one of the Rally cars.

Our dinner at a local restaurant was quiet, and you could see that everyone was mentally preparing for what was to come. A few members of our thirty-one–person team had experienced a Dakar, but many had not. I tried to find out what to expect, but the only often-repeated message I received was to catch some sleep whenever I could, to drink lots of water, and to try not to get killed. Good advice, I thought. As midnight approached, there was much hugging and best wishes for a successful 2012 Dakar, and we all went back to the hotel to get some necessary sleep.

Except for the fireworks. As I walked back to my hotel before the midnight hour, I was wondering why all the clubs and bars around the area, so very busy until the early morning hours on every other night we had been in Mar del Plata, were all closed. New Year's Eve and no bars?

When I opened the curtains in my hotel room, I understood why. Sharply at midnight, fireworks began to be set off all across the city—and not the puny little things we see at home. These were major industrial-grade skyscrapers of light and sound being fired from virtually every backyard and open space I could see. Condo and apartment dwellers were on their balconies, enjoying the show, while the loud bangs from firecrackers kept me on edge. They sounded like gunshots, and in any South American country with a dicey political situation, you can imagine what the sounds of gunfire might mean. Eventually the ruckus died down and, except for the odd yell from a late-night reveler setting off a rogue firecracker, I had a good sleep despite the worries of what the next day—the real beginning to the 2012 Dakar—would bring.

Promptly at 5:45 a.m. the next morning, the motorcycles, called *motos* in Dakar parlance, began to leave the bivouac at the naval base. The departure is very organized, with the first ten competitors in the order they placed in last year's Rally, each departing every two minutes. The next ten *motos* then leave one minute apart, with the following ten every thirty seconds. After that they depart in pairs in thirty-second intervals. This departure plan is designed to give the elite riders at the front of the pack lots of space to not only avoid accidents but also to stay out of the clouds of dust, or what South Americans call *polvo,* thrown up by competitors along the route. Once the *motos* leave, and following a brief pause, the quads depart in the same fashion, followed by the cars and then the trucks. It takes most of the morning to get everyone launched, and to be included in the Dakar standings you must leave the opening day bivouac by just after noon.

For competitors, the Dakar consists of two very different daily routes. The first, which normally begins and ends a race day, is called a "liaison," taking each competitor along regular roads and highways to the beginning of the actual timed section of the race, called a "special," and then along to the next bivouac after the special is completed. Competitors must obey all speed limits and rules of the road during a liaison, and any deviance, including speeding or taking shortcuts, results in significant time penalties for each infraction. It is on the special that the actual racing occurs, and it is the cumulative time through all fourteen of the specials that determines the winner in each category. For the 2012 Dakar, there are 4,408 kilometers of actual racing on specials, but a total of 8,363 kilometers will be traveled overall, including the liaisons at each end of the special race sections. In order to win, or just to finish the Dakar, all specials and liaisons must be completed with the same vehicle and by the same people that started the Rally.

Day one of the 2012 Dakar was, compared to what was to come, a fairly simple but long day. The competitors experienced their first liaison of some 220 kilometers, taking them to the opening special stage, a warm-up, really, of 57 kilometers along the sand and dunes of the Atlantic Coast. Speed was the deciding factor in who won the opening day special, as the terrain to be crossed was relatively unchallenging.

Chaleco Lopez, the top Chilean *moto* rider, took advantage of his fast Aprilia motorcycle to win the day one stage in the *moto* category, moving from fourth position into first. He was followed by Marc Coma in second place, fourteen seconds behind. Thrilling for us was Daniel Gouët's performance, moving up to fifteenth place from where he started in twenty-fifth.

However, this good news was seriously tempered by the tragic death of thirty-eight-year-old Argentinian *moto* rider Jose Martinez Boero, who started the day in 175th position. He crashed at high speed only two kilometers from the end of the stage, suffering serious head and chest injuries. He died of cardiac arrest as he was airlifted to a hospital following heroic efforts by the medical staff who reached him by helicopter only four minutes after the accident.

Boero was competing in only his second Dakar, having retired from the 2011 Rally on day five after becoming hopelessly lost in the sand dunes of the Atacama Desert in northern Chile. Like most privateers, he had made huge personal sacrifice to compete in the Dakar, even selling his apartment in Buenos Aires to finance this latest attempt.

"I'm going to give it everything to get to Lima ... What doesn't kill you strengthens you," he ominously told friends and family in his last Twitter message before starting out. Boero's untimely death was a very sad and somber warning of the significant dangers faced during the Rally.

Following the short special was a very long liaison of some 560 kilometers to the next bivouac in Santa Rosa, La Pampa. Astonishingly, all along the roads and highways we saw people everywhere, cheering and waving. At first I assumed they had all still been up from their New Year's Eve celebrations the night before, especially as the crowds were thick even at five o'clock this morning. But as we drove through the countryside, we realized that all of Argentina had come out to welcome the 2012 Dakar. In every town, at every intersection, and wherever shade from the hot sun could be found, fans were waiting for our passing. They cheered, waved, flew flags, gave us thumbs-up, and voiced their enthusiasm for the entire Dakar. And it was not just the competitors who received this notice. Our truck was also given every welcome, with people waving and running up to us at stoplights, asking for our autographs, and taking our pictures. Can you imagine someone wanting my autograph! It was absolutely crazy.

Argentina is a beautiful country and a mecca for tourists around the world. But there are two important and critical issues any visitor must face, problems that would plague us through all the Argentinian stages of the 2012 Dakar—getting gas and money.

It is challenging to purchase regular gasoline in Argentina. It appears that most vehicles in the country burn something called GNC, a natural gas sold exclusively for cars and trucks. It is much less expensive than normal gasoline, about one-third the price, but filling up can be quite hazardous, and all vehicle occupants are required to vacate their vehicle and stand well away behind a yellow line during the refueling procedure. Oddly, many filling stations sell only this alternative fuel, and gasoline can be difficult to find in some areas.

On our drive west through Argentina, transporting the team to Mar del Plata, on many occasions the search for gasoline became very serious. We would drive to a station that was supposed to sell gas, only to find they were "*sin stock*," out of gasoline. We would obtain directions to other gas stations supposedly well stocked, but at times we would be driving only on fumes before finding available fuel. It was a lesson we learned very early in our drive. Like with motorcycling, when in Argentina, fill up the tank whenever you can. And naturally, also a motorcycling truism, once you have filled up after worrying yourself sick about running out of fuel, you then immediately find five more stations around the next corner with gas to spare.

Another important issue was getting Argentinian currency. Almost everywhere we traveled in the country we discovered that most businesses would only accept cash, and we could find very few that would take a credit card from any financial institution, local or foreign. Apparently the problem started a few years back with a financial crisis faced by the allegedly corrupt Argentinian government. The country was essentially bankrupt, and the government simply gathered all the funds on deposit in all the country's banks for their own account, issuing bonds and a promise to pay, maybe, someday. The banks, in turn, then refused to honor credit card payment requests, as they had no funds to pay them, which forced merchants to stop accepting credit cards from consumers. The practice continues today, with almost all of the restaurants, gas stations, and shops we visited only accepting cash.

Compounding this issue was the problem we encountered finding cash machines that would accept foreign bank or credit cards. Having been forced to borrow Argentinian currency from my team members on the drive to Mar del Plata because I could not get any cash from local ATMs, I was hopeful that in a big tourism center like Mar del Plata, I would readily find sources of currency to repay the loans and fill my coffers for the days we would spend in the outback of the country.

Early one morning as I left the Mar del Plata bivouac, I asked an older couple sitting on the seawall if they knew where I could get some money from an ATM. I thought if I could find a banking center in the city with real international and recognized financial institutions, my luck would change.

The elderly couple thought for a few moments and then said, "Come with us. We will take you there." So off I went with my new friends Carlos and Marta in their little car through the maze of Mar del Plata streets to a financial district where I would hopefully find all the banks.

The drive was most interesting. Most of the streets and intersections in Argentina are distinguished by their lack of stop signs. As my kind and helpful driver, Carlos, approached each intersection, he would only slow down to see who had the right of way. According to some unidentifiable code of conduct, it appeared that drivers who were entering the intersection the fastest, with the loudest horn, or who looked a little crazy, were allowed to pass through first. There was a lot of braking, honking, accelerating, and weaving employed to safely navigate these intersections, but somehow it all seemed to work. As a gringo used to the government and police telling me where and when to stop and go, it was a bit nerve-racking.

And, despite finding major international banking names, I still had problems getting access to my bank accounts both in Chile and in Canada. After visiting four bank ATMs, I was finally successful, and the kind Argentinian couple drove me back to the bivouac. I gave them each a Canada pin.

As we drove along the day one liaison to the Santa Rosa bivouac, I noticed numerous shrines built alongside the roads and highways. Some were small and nondescript, others quite large and well maintained, covered with flags and bunting, and including statues of saints or the Blessed Virgin, with candles burning and sometimes even strings of colored lights powered ingeniously by pirated electricity from nearby electrical poles. I assumed these shrines were placed to honor friends or family who might have died in an accident at that location, but many strangely had huge mountains of empty soft drink and water bottles piled around them. What was that about?

"They are called *animitas*," Rodrigo explained to me. "And you are correct, they are normally built to honor a relative who, typically, met a tragic end at or near the location of their shrine. The family will visit the *animita* on the relative's birthday and other major holidays, especially on New Year's Eve, an important day to meet with the soul of one's lost family member."

"But what about the empty pop bottles?" I asked. "Is this some tribute to the god of recycling?"

Rodrigo then told me the story of the Difunta Correa, a heroine in South American culture, and in whose honor many of these shrines are constructed. Legend has it that Doña Correa, an impoverished mother, was wandering in the foothills of the Andes with her newborn daughter. Begging for some water for her child from a wealthy landowner, she was cruelly refused and sent on her way. That night, caught in a freak winter storm, the mother succumbed to the cold weather and, most importantly for the myth, a lack of water. However, her daughter, feeding at her mother's breast, was able to remain alive and was soon rescued. An *animita* was then erected at the site in memory of the mother's heroism. As the story of the child's near-death experience and the sacrifice of her mother spread, further shrines to the Difunta Correa began appearing. The practice of leaving bottles at the shrines soon became popular, ensuring the mother's spirit has sufficient water, pop, or other drinks in her afterlife.

For competitors in the Dakar, having sufficient water is one of the most important regulations, and participants are checked numerous times to ensure each is carrying a specified amount of water at all times during the Rally. There have been numerous incidents of dehydration during the Dakar, some quite serious, as competitors suffer through daily temperatures in the high 40°C. Let's hope this year's Dakar would see no shrines built to memorialize a competitor who, like the Difunta Correa, meets a tragic end from a lack of fluids.

In addition to the *animitas*, the Dakar organization had also placed a number of their control vehicles along the highways to monitor speeds and adherence to traffic laws. The ASO has radar detectors, the facility to see what each vehicle's Tripy is recording in real time, and to take pictures of any offense. We were very careful, using cruise control to ensure we did not speed. Oddly, the only vehicles that passed us at velocities clearly over the speed limit were ASO organization cars. I guess if you run the event, you can do what you want. We thought of taking pictures of the offenders but decided it might not be very wise to bite the hand that feeds us.

As gasoline is challenging to find in Argentina, there are designated fuel stations along the Dakar route for participants to use, with security and highway police employed to stop traffic and keep the crowds controlled. These gas stations were powerful magnets for fans, with crowds surrounding the pump area to see their favorites up close. The stations are also an excellent opportunity for support vehicles to wait should the competitors need anything or encounter problems.

At one station I watched Chilean motorcycle star Francisco López Contardo talk calmly to a mother and child and then have his picture taken with the kid on his lap. Born in 1975, Lopez began riding motorcycles at the age of four, and by 1989 he was winning Latin American and global off-road championships. He won his first Dakar stage in 2009, a true Chilean hero as the Rally had entered his country for the first time, and in 2010, he placed third overall in the motorcycle category. He started fourth in this year's Dakar, competing for the Italian motorcycle company Aprilia.

Like most people in South America, Lopez is known best by his nickname *Chaleco*. It seems that almost everyone uses a short form for their given names—called an *apodo*. These *apodos* are much more than nicknames; they can actually replace the proper given name of a person and how they are known. You will be introduced to many people named *Pancho* or *Pancha* (depending on the gender, and not *poncho*, the blanket you wear over your head on a cool evening), *Pato* (it also translates as "duck," but in a much different sense), *Flaco* ("skinny," "tall," or both), *Pipe*, *Pedro*, *Lucho*, *Cote*, and a host of others. Proper nicknames, in the North American sense, are also used. For example, you can call your slightly overweight best friend *Gordo*, which means "fat," but in this sense it is most often a term of affection.

Another similar term of affection is *huevón*, though this *apodo* can have a very different connotation when used in different contexts. The word's literal translation is "big egg," and it can be used as a term of friendship in a greeting, similar to our slang for "buddy" or "pal." But it can also be an expression of anger or disgust—someone is an idiot, a fool, a buffoon. For us gringos, confusion reigns supreme, as the word *huevón* is close to the Spanish word for egg (*huevo*) and for the male testicle (*hueva*). My wife once ordered scrambled *heuvas* for breakfast, so, in addition to asking for smashed-up male testicles instead of eggs, she potentially may have been calling our waiter a big fat fool.

But the *apodo* becomes confusing in Lopez's case. Roughly translated into English, *Chaleco* means "vest" or "sweater," and apparently refers to the same name given to his father, Renato, who was a three-time Chilean national motocross champion and who always raced wearing a woolen vest knitted by his wife. But really, calling a top motorcycle competitor "sweater"? One motorcycling friend of mine calls his longtime riding companion *Brutus*. Now that is a good strong name for a guy who rides motorcycles!

And Lopez is tough. In early May 2011, during a warm-up Rally for the Dakar in Tunisia, Lopez was thrown from his motorcycle just short of the finish line. He suffered lung damage, a pulmonary edema, fractures to his tibia, fibula, ribs, shoulder, hands, and feet, as well as fractures to his skull and spine. He was in intensive care for weeks. But only seven months later, here he is competing in his fourth South American Dakar. Clearly, calling this guy *Chaleco* is a term of respect and maybe, just maybe, this *chaleco* is bulletproof.

CHAPTER FOUR
A BIVOUAC IS A VERY NOISY PLACE

Our first long day of driving was a test as to how we would all get along together in our little truck. Our Honda Ridgeline was huge, as pickup trucks go, but with the three of us in the cab, along with much of Rodrigo's very valuable photography equipment and our own stuff sitting on one of the backseats, there was not a lot of personal space. The back bed of the pickup held all of our bags containing our clothing, our tents and sleeping bags, the extra fuel tanks we would need, the required safety equipment, and a lot of other crap that accumulates on a road trip, all protected by a locking cover.

After the three-day trip from Santiago with Rodrigo, there were now three of us in our truck, as Pedro, Daniel's father, had finally joined us in Mar del Plata.

Daniel came to his love of motorcycles through his father. Pedro is a senior executive with one of Chile's top forestry companies and, with Daniel's two sisters, lives in Concepción, about five hours south of Santiago on Chile's Pacific coast. He is an intense, serious man, and while his command of English is not that extensive, he and I were working hard at communicating.

Pedro has ridden motorcycles since he was a young man and now has interests in two Honda dealerships in Concepción. Before the Dakar began, I visited the Gouet family at their home, riding my motorcycle south from our home near Santiago. Pedro and four of his friends and nephews met me a few hours north of Concepción to guide me to their home, and they were all excellent motorcycle riders. The fact that I had trouble keeping up with them I can only attribute to their having more powerful bikes than me. Or not.

Rodrigo and Pedro could not be further apart on the political spectrum. In South America, the terms "right wing" and "left wing" really do demarcate attitudes and beliefs. While we in North America may blur the distinction and move perhaps closer to the middle of political ideology, in South America how you position yourself politically can truly define who you are.

During the hours together traveling to Santa Rosa, I listened as best I could to very heated discussions between my two traveling companions about a number of issues—the environment, the search for much needed sources of electrical power in Chile, recent election results, the rescue of the twenty-one miners in northern Chile a few months before we left, and other controversial topics. It seemed like there was nothing the two could agree upon, and for our long hours together each would try to convince the other that their position was right. Interestingly, no angry words were exchanged, no fights broke out, and both appeared to respect the other's opinion, no matter how wrong they thought the other was. These heated conversations would continue through most of our days together, but fortunately only when the two of them were in the front of the truck together. The backseat was reserved for catching some sleep.

The downside to these discussions came after we had stopped; each would come to me to privately explain how naive or misguided my other companion was, and to try to solicit my support to win the battle. Understanding that I would be in close quarters with these two people in our cab truck for two weeks, I realized taking any side would be a big mistake. In the interests of traveling in peace, I simply told each combatant that I was a stupid gringo and in no position to comment on what was occurring in their country. For some reason this evasion did not stop them from trying to convince me. It would be an interesting time together.

And then there were the times they talked about me, believing I was asleep or I did not understand their Spanish. Midway through the first day, I heard them mention "the Gringo" in a talk, and then they both laughed, sharing some kind of joke at my expense. I was resting and my eyes were closed, but I knew they were referring to me.

In the brief moment of silence as their laughter died down, I said, in a quiet but firm tone, "*Concha su madre.*" This phrase is by far the worst insult you can say to anyone in Chile, and it is disgustingly rude.

They both turned around to look at me, astonishment on their faces.

"Have you been listening to us? Have you understood what we are saying? Where the hell did you learn that insult?" they both asked in unison.

I just smiled and closed my eyes again. It was the last time I heard them laughing about their pet gringo.

We reached our first real Dakar bivouac outside the town of Santa Rosa, La Pampa, in the early evening of New Year's Day after the long 763-kilometer drive from Mar del Plata. Our two huge Tamarugal transport trucks were in place, and all four race motorcycles were being serviced. The riders were showering, studying the route for the next day, or having a massage. A surprisingly decent dinner of roast chicken, pasta, and watermelon was served for everyone in big tents, with a hospitality center nearby offering beer, wine, light snacks, and everything made with Red Bull. Karcher, the company that makes power washers, provided free cleaning for all race vehicles, a real boon after the hot dusty roads the competitors faced in day one's 40°C heat.

Following my quick dinner, I went to the media center only to find I was supposed to have subscribed for Internet access from the ASO for the exorbitant cost of some three thousand pounds for 10 mgs of upload. A few pictures and I would be into them for even more money. I then discovered the "Web Centre," where you can access their computers, connected to the Internet, for one pound per minute, but they close at 9:00 p.m. I talked to Rodrigo, and he explained that almost everyone in South America has an open Wi-Fi network—restaurants, gas stations, and shops—and it was even possible to just sit outside certain houses to pick up an open signal. So now I was a signal bandit, grabbing a table whenever we stopped for gas or a break and stealing their Internet access.

A Dakar bivouac makes quite a presence. Approximately two to three acres in size, they are typically located on the edge of the designated town or city, using whatever large flat spot is available. For the 2012 Dakar, bivouacs were established on racetracks, close to military bases, within airport landing strips, on large parking lots, and in any clear desert area. In order to ensure the sites are ready and available, the ASO moves two bivouacs ahead of whatever current location is being used, with the next location entirely ready and the third in preparation. Logistically, the organization uses seventy-eight cars, ten trucks, eleven helicopters, seven large airplanes, fifteen buses, and fifteen transport trucks to move everyone and everything around.

At one end of the bivouac are the various services necessary to run an efficient Rally. There is a large U-shaped, tented catering area containing rows of picnic tables where we would all share our evening and morning meals, and pick up our boxed lunches and water for the day. Also located in this section of the bivouac is the large medical center, where doctors and nurses are available twenty-four hours a day to treat any ailment or concern. Showers and outdoor toilets are in a separate area close by, one for men and one for women. The press has access to a separate tent that only accredited participants can use, providing us with Internet access and bulletins detailing the latest results and standings.

In another tented area, normally in front of the catering section, the ASO provides daily video updates of that day's stage, along with other coverage of interest to Rally participants. The driver briefings for the next day's special stages, similar to the one I attended before the podium celebrations in Mar del Plata, normally occur from a raised platform attached to this video zone. The organizers also take up space at this end of the bivouac to hear protests and deal with the myriad of issues that crop up during the Dakar. Included at this end of the bivouac are various hospitality tents provided by sponsors such as Red Bull, as well as large event centers and receptions provided by each host country, usually featuring local entertainment, information about the country, along with typical foods and drinks. These host country pavilions are very popular within the bivouac, and are often the only place to escape the dust and wind and enjoy a local beer or glass of wine.

The rest of the bivouac, approximately two-thirds of the enclosed area, is reserved for competitors' compounds. Generally on a "first come, first serve" basis, each team grabs sufficient space to set up their assistance trucks, an area for repair and maintenance, and for the individual tents to be installed for everyone to spend the night. Often teams will send one truck ahead early each morning to grab a choice location within the next bivouac. This strategy can also be important if, like our Tamarugal team, you are racing both motorcycles and cars. The bikes leave very early in the morning and can arrive at the next bivouac in the early afternoon, and it is critical to have space set up for them so the riders can rest and have their *motos* serviced.

When the assistance trucks arrive at the bivouac, there is an attempt to guide the vehicles into grids to ensure there is some kind of road access between the team compounds for safe vehicle access. However, as the teams flood into the area, the best laid plans collapse quickly, resulting in a myriad of winding paths and roads between the hundreds of trucks and race vehicles. All told, there are some three thousand people housed within the bivouac. It is quite something.

At first I wondered why many teams quickly installed flags sporting readily identifiable logos on the roofs of their trucks. During my first night in the Santa Rosa bivouac, I found out why.

Being a gentleman of a certain age, I need to visit the bathroom in the middle of most nights, but, after my ablutions and walking out of the latrine area, I could not remember exactly where our compound was located. As I peered into the confusion of bright arc lights, swirling dust, and noise, I had no idea where I had been sleeping. I walked in the general direction of the back end of the bivouac until I finally located the familiar Tamarugal flag flying on top of one of our supply trucks. As I crawled back into my sleeping bag, I told myself how I must be more diligent about our location within future bivouacs so as not to waste any of my scarce and valuable sleep time.

Another aspect I discovered on my first night's emergency run to the bathroom was the tight security under which I would be living for the next two week. Each bivouac is enclosed by high fences with local police and military personnel patrolling the perimeter by foot and in a fleet of special cars and 4WD trucks, as well as overhead in helicopters to ensure only authorized vehicles and participants have access to the people and expensive equipment that make up the Dakar. The ASO had learned its lessons in Africa, where things frequently went missing and, more importantly, where they were the object of terrorist attacks. Thus, security is taken very seriously—each vehicle has a coded chip affixed to the windshield that allows access, as did each of our name badges, and woe betide the person found without an approved and functioning name badge!

The competitor's section of the bivouac is alive with noise and activity all night. Once the sun goes down, awnings and umbrellas are replaced by bright arc lights on tall poles illuminating each team's area. Work continues from when the *motos*, cars, and trucks arrive from the day's racing to when they leave again on the next day's stage. The work ranges from simple fuel, oil, filter, and tire replacements with checks and adjustments of everything else, to complete overhauls. You can sense the urgency in certain compounds as teams of mechanics converse quietly crowding around a vehicle.

For the many months before the Dakar begins, the mechanics and drivers spend a great deal of time preparing and confirming checklists for daily maintenance duties, both before a vehicle leaves a bivouac for that day's race stages and when they return in the evening. It is an extensive list, including everything from oil levels through differential checks to inspections of the frames for cracks. For example, I learned that three replacement windshields for each car were being carried, as they underwent a lot of abuse.

The team also prepared tool lists, including who would carry what tools and supplies. Some essential tools would be included with each race car and motorcycle during the specials when no help could be provided, while others would be on assistance vehicles should issues arise on the liaison drives. The rest, along with the majority of spare parts, would be carried by our two large transport trucks to await arrival at each bivouac. The two Rally cars on the Tamarugal team were being supported by the three mechanics who had built the vehicles in California. The motorcyclists each have their own mechanic and tool kit carried on the big transport trucks and assistance vehicles. The bike pilots and their mechanics have worked together for some time and are an integrated and close team.

It is fascinating to watch and listen to the discussions between the drivers and riders and their mechanics. Hand gestures are a key to communications, as are "back of napkin" drawings. They all use acronyms (I now know that a "CV" is a constant velocity joint), and strange nomenclature flows through their discussions like a foreign language—valves, pins, shafts, filters, connectors, cables, pans, frames, lug nuts, and many others. Numerical adjustments and changes to settings in both metric and imperial measures are reviewed and gone over in great detail.

Preparing these checklists and tool manifests is crucial for all teams, but particularly for the many solo, one-person competitors. A number of primarily *moto* competitors are participating in the Dakar on their own, challenging themselves to see if they can just finish a Dakar. The organization allows them to pack one large plastic box with everything they can fit—clothes, tools, and spare parts—and the ASO carries it for them from bivouac to bivouac. Fortunately, it really is a collegial atmosphere in the bivouac, and these privateers are often adopted by the bigger teams, helping with tools and parts when they get in trouble. But it is odd to see the huge team compounds surrounded by large transport trucks loaded with supplies, along with comfortable tents and mattresses for the crew, and next door is a single guy wearing his riding clothes, lying on the ground beside his bike, trying to get some sleep before the next day's departure.

Speaking of tents, the Tamarugal team had provided a tent and mattress for everyone, packed on their big trucks. However, the tent labeled with my name was broken and useless. I decided to sleep that first night in the back of our truck to make sure I was off the ground so no creepy crawling things could get at me. I am terrified of spiders, and South America has quite a few, including the large tarantula-like beast they call the "little chicken." These big eight-legged hairy items are not poisonous, but I really did not want to confront one in my sleeping bag as I zipped in for the night.

The truck bed was quite comfortable, and the sides shielded me from the bright lights in the mechanics' work area. I looked up at the unfamiliar southern hemisphere solar system and tried to sleep.

But it was noisy, so very, very noisy. The low growl of diesel generators found in all team compounds was punctuated by the whine of drills, the rattle of pneumatic wrenches, the scream of air compressors and power washers, the deep pounding of hammers on steel and iron, and the bleep of powerful, high-performance motorcycle engines being revved up, all accompanied in multichannel sound by the deep growl of powerful truck engines uninhibited by mufflers that drain horsepower. All of this noise was accentuated by the smell of engine exhaust, gasoline, and solvents. It was a very busy place.

In 1914, British journalist Julian Street visited Detroit and described the energy of the Ford Motor Company's Highland Park factory:

> The whole room, with its interminable aisles, its whirling shafts and wheels, its forest of roof-supporting posts and flapping, flying leather belting, its endless rows of writhing machinery, its shrieking, hammering, and clatter, its smell of oil, its autumn haze of smoke, its savage-looking foreign population—to my mind it expressed one thing and that was delirium … Fancy a jungle of wheels and belts and weird iron forms—of men, machinery and movement—add to it every kind of sound you can imagine: the sound of a million squirrels chirping, a million monkeys quarreling, a million lions roaring, a million pigs dying, a million elephants smashing through a forest of sheet iron, a million boys whistling on their fingers, a million others coughing with the whopping cough, a million sinners groaning as they are dragged to hell—imagine all of this happening at the very edge of Niagara falls, with the everlasting roar of the cataract as a perpetual background, and you may acquire a vague conception of that place.

Street's description of Henry Ford's first factory perfectly depicts living in a Dakar bivouac.

Just as I was starting to doze off, around 2:00 a.m., one of the two Tamarugal cars finally arrived in the compound, and the noise and smells really started in earnest, as there were significant problems. The crew started ripping the car apart and working on everything they could find. It took them all night.

When I woke up at four thirty the next morning (I told you we started early at the Dakar), I approached Rick, one of the car mechanics. "I know the cars are important, but really, did you have to wreck my sleep all night?"

He looked at me, saw I was joking, and advised, with a grin, that if you did not have a sense of humor, you would not make it past day three of the Dakar Rally. Rick's sense of humor would be severely tested later that morning when he learned one of his two cars had been abandoned in the outback early in the previous day's stage and was forced to withdraw from the Dakar with a blown engine.

Day two was a more typical Dakar day. The liaison section was 487 kilometers, taking the competitors to the start of the special just outside Algarrobo del Aguila in western Argentina, approaching the east side of the Andes Mountains. The 295 kilometers of the special began quickly as high speeds were attained over the relatively solid and rocky tracks through the pampas. However, midway through and continuing to the end of the stage, competitors' speeds were reduced in the more technical sections of sand and dunes, particularly in the Reserva Provincial Laguna de Llncenalo along the Sierra Nevado mountains. Here, in an area Argentinians call Nihuil, the sand is gray-colored and very slippery, a result of intense volcanic activity several thousand years in the past. A number of riders crashed in the soft sand, taking quite a few out of the competition. After this tricky special, a short highway ride took competitors to the next bivouac in San Rafael.

We left the Santa Rosa bivouac shortly after 5:00 a.m. once Daniel had departed for his day two ride. The plan was to drive to the finish area about sixty kilometers before the next bivouac in San Rafael, and hopefully there would be a spectator area set up where we could watch the *motos* finish.

Leaving Santa Rosa, we drove for what seemed forever through the pampas of Argentina, low flat scrub land where huge parcels are used for raising and grazing cattle. It is a beautiful and difficult landscape, but there sure isn't much there. As we drove east and north, nearing the foothills of the Andes, the flat and arid landscape was transformed into the more familiar vineyards and acres of olive orchards. Many of the roads were lined on both sides by tall columnar deciduous trees called Alamos, providing welcome shade for us and the spectators in the over forty-degree heat. The flickering sunlight, dappled through the leaves of the tall trees, provided new light on the local scenery after the harsh glare of the open pampas.

Navigating the Dakar is a fascinating logistics exercise. Months before the Rally begins, the teams from the ASO travel extensively throughout South America, finding and then mapping the special stages for that year's race. How they find and get to some of these areas is a mystery, but using local guides and a fleet of helicopters, they locate and map what is some of the most challenging terrain in the world. The finalized special routes are kept under lock and key until the night before each race day, and competitors are forbidden to explore the area in and around the expected routes prior to the Rally.

Once the specials are determined, the ASO then maps out the liaison routes, as well as the location for each night's bivouac. All of this information is then translated into a number of languages and downloaded into the proprietary Tripy systems and the most important "Roadbook."

The Roadbook is by far the most important tool for a competitor because the Dakar is much more than a race. It is also a highly elaborate and demanding orienteering exercise that challenges every participant's navigational skills. Mistakes can cost valuable time, the difference between winning and losing, and can often result in accidents that force competitors out of contention.

Each night competitors receive a new Roadbook for the following day. In text and using a comprehensive set of more than 120 different symbols, the next day's route over the timed special is described in extensive detail, including warnings of hazards and landmarks to follow that guide the racers to the various on-route checkpoints and refueling centers.

As you can see on the next page, the Roadbook lexicon is complicated, and all the various symbols must be memorized and understood. It can mean the difference in finishing a Rally, or even surviving a Rally.

The detail in the Roadbook is astonishing and can show route changes in as short a distance as a tenth of a kilometer or less. Car and truck competitors are issued a Roadbook in booklet form, while motorcyclists are given a paper scroll that fits into a special rectangular holder riding high on the front of their handlebar. You can imagine the concentration it must take for a *moto* rider to follow the Roadbook while watching an odometer to measure distance traveled while at the same time watching for mandated waypoints and traveling as fast as possible, avoiding road hazards and other race vehicles.

Symbol	Code (FR)	Code (EN)		Symbol	FR	EN		Code	FR	EN
▶	ROUTE	ROAD		〜〜	OUED	OUED / WADI		GV	GRAVIER	GRAVEL
▶	ROUTE avec separation	DUAL CARRIAGEWAY		⊄	LANGUE DE SABLE	SAND SPIT		G/D	GAUCHE / DROITE	LEFT / RIGHT
→	PISTE TRACÉE	TRACK		⌂	BORNE	KILOMETRE MARKER		D/G	DROITE / GAUCHE	RIGHT / LEFT
---▶	HORS PISTE	OFF TRACK		森	CIMETIÈRE	CEMETERY		MVS	MAUVAIS	BAD
!	ATTENTION	1 DANGER		○	PUIT	BARREL		EMP	EMPIERRE	STONY OR ROCKY
!!	DANGER	2 DANGER		⌐┐	PANNEAU	SIGNPOST		DEF	DEFONCE	ROUGH
!!!	GROS DANGER	3 DANGER		⊠	MAISON	HOUSE		ORN	ORNIERE	RUT
∽	CUVETTE	DIP		⌐	FORT	FORT		SER	SERRE	TIGHT
⌒	BOSSE	BUMP		L	POTEAU / POULET	POST		HP	HORS PISTE	OFF PISTE / OFF TRACK
⌂	COMPRESSION	COMPRESSION		⌐○	IMGI	TYRE		HP'	HORS PISTE INTERDIT	OFF TRACK FORBIDDEN
∽	SAIGNEE	DITCH		⌐	PUIT	WELL		OUED	OUED	OUED / WADI
⌐	RADIER	STEP		⌐	DUNES silhouette à dessiner	DUNES individual to draw each		E3	E TROIT	NARROW
⌐	MARCHE EN DESCENTE	STEP DOWN		⌒⌒	MONTAGNE silhouette à dessiner	MOUNTAIN individual drawing for each		DS	DANS	IN
⌐	MARCHE EN MONTEE	STEP UP		(DZ) (FZ)	DEBUT de Zone / FIN de Zone vitesse limitee	START of Zone / END of Zone controlled speed		IMP	IMPERATIF	IMPERATIVE
↘	DESCENTE	DOWNHILL		(80) (70)	Limite de VITESSE	SPEED LIMIT		QT	QUITTER	LEAVE
↗	MONTEE	UPHILL		STOP	STOP	STOP		G^D	GRAND	BIG
⌐	TROU EFFONDRE	HOLE COLLAPSE		⌐	DEVERS	CAMBER		NBX	NOMBREUX	MANY
⌂	ORNIERE	RUTS		⊘	DEPART	START		RLT	RALENTIR	SLOW DOWN
∽	ONDULATION DIVISIBLE	UNDULATION		⊘	ARRIVEE	FINISH		±V	PLUS OU MOINS VISIBLE	MORE or LESS VISIBLE
⌒	SUR PONT / SOUS PONT	ABOVE BRIDGE / UNDER BRIDGE		⊙	CHRONO	CLOCK		S	SINUEUX	TWISTY
⌐	GUE	FORD		⊙	ESSENCE	FUEL		PP	PISTE PRINCIPALE	MAIN TRACK
◎	TROU	HOLE		(PH)	PHOTO	PHOTO		TD	TOUT DROIT	KEEP STRAIGHT
⌐	CASE	CASES		⊘	CP	CP		RO	ROUTE	ROAD
⌂	CITERNE	WATER TANK		⊘	DEBUT ZONE D'ASSISTANCE	START of ASSISTANCE ZONE		TDSPP	TOUT DROIT SUR PISTE PRINCIPALE	KEEP STRAIGHT ON MAIN TRACK
⌂	FIL BARBELE	BARBED WIRE FENCE		⊗	FIN ZONE D'ASSISTANCE	END of ASSISTANCE ZONE		TDRPP	TOUT DROIT SUR ROUTE PRINCIPALE	KEEP STRAIGHT ON MAIN ROAD
∼∼∼	CLOTURE	FENCE		V	VILLAGE	VILLAGE		P//	PISTES PARALLELES	PARALLEL TRACKS
⊥⊥⊥	LIGNE ELECTRIQUE	ELECTRIC LINE		(WPM)	WAYPOINT MASQUE	WAYPOINT MASKED		P	PISTE	TRACK
⌒⌒	DUNES	DUNES		(WPE)	WAYPOINT ECLIPSE	WAYPOINT ECLIPSE		C	CAP	BEARING
⌐	DUNETTE	SMALL DUNE		AD	A DROITE	ON THE RIGHT		TJS	TOUJOURS	ALWAYS
🌴	PALMIER	PALM TREE		AG	A GAUCHE	ON THE LEFT		VG	VEGETATION	VEGETATION
⊥	ANTENNE	ANTENNA / MAST		D	DROITE	RIGHT		CX	CAILLOUX	STONE
□-□	PORTE / BARRIERE	GATE BARRIER		G	GAUCHE	LEFT		EFF	EFFONDRE	COLLAPSED
				SA	SABLE	SAND		RP	REPRISE REFERENCE	TO TAKE
DNT	DUNETTE	SMALL DUNE		DN	DUNE	DUNE		BETW	ENTRE	BETWEEN

The Dakar introduced Roadbooks to replace the standard consumer GPS that have become so popular today. Many riders in the past were using these GPS systems and coordinates as guides only and were driving as fast as possible in a straight line between waypoints without heed for dangers on the route. A number of accidents had occurred as drivers launched themselves over cliffs or into rock faces, and the Rally organizers decided to eliminate the GPS directional system by forcing competitors to travel along predetermined routes to make the Rally more challenging, safer, and to create a more level playing field for all competitors.

To ensure competitors more or less adhere to the proscribed route on each special, the ASO had installed a proprietary GPS system on each vehicle during the registration period in Mar del Plata. The system was described to me as a large digital compass that includes an odometer and speed registration function. When each competitor is within three kilometers of what is called a "WPS," or way safety point, the location is displayed on the GPS to ensure each vehicle drives through the WPS. Each WPS must be crossed within twenty meters of its defined location. These safety points are often used to demarcate a town or area where speed must be reduced, or also to warn of a substantial hazard ahead like a deep ditch or steep descent down a hill.

The ASO GPS system also displays what they call a "WPE," or waypoint eclipse, each appearing on the digital compass when a vehicle is within two hundred meters. These WPEs are generally navigational challenges and must also be crossed within a specified distance, normally twenty meters. If a WPE is missed, the time penalties can be severe—as high as two hours in some cases. WPEs can be located at the bottom of a series of sand dunes, for example. One competitor told me he knew he was at such a WPE by all the other vehicles stuck and looking around for help. They also appear on the GPS when navigating across flat land as a way to make sure no one cuts corners too soon. We watched examples of this function at a number of spectator areas where all the race vehicles appeared to turn at exactly the same otherwise unidentifiable point.

In addition, the ASO GPS system includes a bailout signal. If a competitor is really lost, they can call control and ask for the day's code. By entering this code into the GPS, it will reveal all of that day's WPE locations, providing a defined direction for the vehicle to get back on track and finish the stage. However, utilizing this feature incurs significant time penalties, and if you use it more than twice, you are disqualified from the Dakar. All vehicles are prohibited from using any other type of GPS system on pain of disqualification.

The other essential tool used in conjunction with the Roadbook and the ASO GPS are the *terratrip* systems installed on most race vehicles. These are sophisticated odometers used to navigate in conjunction with the mileage details in the Roadbook and the GPS that chart the route to be taken during a race day. As the Roadbooks are very accurate—calibrated to as little as a tenth of a kilometer—the *terratrips* also need to be very accurate. In the past, two were used by the top auto teams with one attached to each axle. When the Dakar cars were rear-wheel drive, the front axle *terratrip* was the most important, as the rear wheels could spin in the sand, wreaking havoc with accuracy. But with the advent of 4WD vehicles, this wheel spinning can occur with both axles. There is also the issue of vehicles frequently going airborne as they race at high speeds over uneven terrain. Today, two *terratrip* systems are employed to ensure greater accuracy along with the proprietary Dakar GPS system, with one *terratrip* normally counting total mileage on a special and the second measuring distance between Roadbook points. On motorcycles, the second odometer is reset at each Roadbook point with a thumb switch on the left-hand grip of the handlebar.

Each *terratrip* and ASO GPS system is also equipped with a reset switch. When the navigator or motorcycle rider notices that the *terratrip* or GPS is out of synch with the Roadbook at a major and obvious point—a stage checkpoint, for example—it can be reset to zero and the car or bike can follow the mileage data in the Roadbook from that point forward, as the details in the Roadbook also include the distance between each waypoint.

I thought using a compass was challenging. A friend once called the science of orienteering, more appropriately, *dis*-orienteering.

As an "assistance vehicle," we were not issued Roadbooks, but our Tripy was our guide and mentor for the entire Dakar route. It took us places we would never find on a map or with a conventional GPS system—except today.

As we were filling up with gas close to San Rafael, our bivouac destination for the night, one of the ASO vehicles pulled in beside us. Our Tripy GPS system did not include the race routes, only the assistance routes, and we were not sure where the finish of that day's stage was located. We knew it was near the town of El Nihuil, but our maps were not clear, and it looked like a complicated route to get there.

The young Frenchman driving the ASO truck, accompanied by two television photographers from NBC, said he was headed to the finish area and we could follow him. Finally we would have official papal blessing to exceed the speed limit, and did we fly. The highway turned into a beautiful but poorly maintained road that wound through the lovely Rio Atuel valley the locals call Valle Grande. It was lined with some pretty, and some not-so-pretty, hotels and hostels, as well as rock climbing and river rafting, which looked like fun on the fast-moving currents.

The road eventually narrowed, turning into loose stone, gravel, and sand, winding up a steep hill in a series of switchbacks to the top of a large hydroelectric dam that had created a beautiful deep-blue lake on one side. We stopped for some pictures and a chat, and then climbed back into our trucks to continue the ascent up and away from the lake. Once past the dam we were confronted by handmade signs in Spanish warning us the road ahead was under construction. But the Tripy in the ASO truck we were following said to continue, so off we went.

The road surface deteriorated significantly as we continued to climb into the cordillera. A grader had tried to smooth things out, unsuccessfully, and only making matters worse by narrowing the navigable path even further. There were no guardrails or shoulders, only steep, steep drops down sheer cliffs into the river valley below.

And then we hit our first landslide. Part of the hill had come down and covered the road with boulders and rocks. Clearly someone had climbed over the fallen rubble before us, so we inched our way across. The ASO vehicle had an easier time, as it was much higher than our Honda Ridgeline. The bottom of our chassis scraped alarmingly a number of times, but we got across only to find a worse rock slide around the next corner. We managed to traverse that one and then a third. When we encountered a fourth pile of rubble blocking our way, we decided to look around the next corner, only to find complete sections of the road ahead washed out by massive piles of rock and sand.

With a typical Gallic shrug of his shoulders, the French driver stated we could go no farther. We had to turn around and head back, following our Tripy navigation toward the next bivouac, missing that day's stage completion.

But I heard another great Spanish phrase during this route. What we call "speed bumps" on roads they call *lomo de toro*, or "the meat of bulls." I'm not sure why. Maybe it refers to the lump on the back of a bull, but it sounds great.

Later that night, we learned the Dakar had suffered another series of bad accidents. A French motorcycle rider moving swiftly through the special had collided with a cow at an estimated 150 kilometers an hour. His *moto* was completely destroyed, the cow was in a few pieces, and the rider was in a coma in the San Rafael hospital. In another incident, two Dakar spectators—a father and son—were killed when their ultralight airplane crashed while following the day two special stage. These tragic events were further reminders of just how dangerous the Dakar could be.

Daniel had a good day two, finishing in nineteenth position on the special and sitting overall in seventeenth place, a strong improvement from his starting position at number twenty-five. We would head north tomorrow through Mendoza and up the eastern side of the Andes to San Juan, Argentina.

CHAPTER FIVE
PREPARING FOR A DAKAR IS LIKE GOING TO WAR

"*Hey, Gringo, algo de ayuda por favor.*"

My new name—*el gringo*—was being used affectionately, most of the time, I believed—although the tag could be tinged with a bit of contempt by South Americans when referring to their North American neighbors. We *were* different in North America, we often didn't understand our neighbors to the south, and we could find their ways of doing things bureaucratic, time consuming, and endlessly frustrating. South Americans, in turn, found our lack of patience, our hurry, our pace, and our sense of immediacy all a bit too much. I remember the lawyer who managed the drawn-out purchase of our home in Chile, giving me the best piece of advice I had received when adapting to life in South America: "Never say, 'We don't do things that way at home,'" he told us with some authority. "Because we don't."

I evoke this sage bit of wisdom whenever I am in South America, confronted by long lines of people waiting to do anything or having to deal with two or three people to make a purchase, businesses being closed for siestas in the afternoon for indeterminable times, banks being open from only 10:00 a.m. to 2:00 p.m., with some time away from their desks for lunch, of course, and the lack of an appreciation for being on time. When you invite someone for dinner, say, at seven thirty, you can expect them anytime between eight and midnight. We call it "Chile time."

Over the last two weeks of December, I had spent a few days with the Tamarugal team at their staging location in Lampa, north of Santiago, getting to know some of the guys. I got quite used to being asked to come by, say, around 10:00 a.m. and not have anyone else turn up until 11:00. After five years in Chile, I was quite accustomed to their sense of time.

Team Tamarugal was fielding two cars and four motorcycles in the 2012 Dakar. Javier Campillay, the son of the main sponsor of the team, was driving the first car. A handsome young man and father of three, Javier had competed in all three previous South American Dakars. In addition to his focus on competing in the Rally, I noticed how involved he was in his family business throughout the weeks of the Rally, spending each evening in the bivouacs tethered to his BlackBerry and cell phone. His navigator and copilot, Juan Pablo Rodriguez, is a highly experienced competitor who has participated in a number of Rallies, both as a driver and navigator. The second Tamarugal car was being driven by Carlo de Gavardo, copiloted by his navigator, Eduardo Blanco. Carlo is one of Chile's most renowned Rally Raid participants, having competed in numerous Dakars and other Rally Raids both on motorcycles and in cars. He is a hero to many Chileans, and would be closely watched.

Both Javier and Carlo became good friends during the Rally, helping me understand the complexity of their cars and the challenges they faced. Dedicated and experienced, their enthusiasm for Rally Raid and the Dakar was infectious. They also possessed a keen sense of humor and were constantly ribbing me about being a gringo in South America, a source of good-hearted ridicule throughout the continent.

The Tamarugal motorcycle team was composed of my new friend Daniel Gouët; the *Hermanos Prohens* (two brothers), Felipe and Jaime, who had competed together in Rally Raids for many years; and the youngest member of the *moto* team, Claudio Rodriguez, nicknamed "Burro" for his stubbornness. Each *moto* rider and his crew had been working on their individual motorcycles for months, getting ready for the Dakar. My wife told me the Tamarugal *moto* team was comprised of the most handsome men in the Dakar field, and the attention they received from legions of women along the route attested to her good taste.

Filling out the team were the support truck drivers and mechanics; a physiotherapist skilled in massage; publicists; and many others. In total, there were thirty-one of us who made our way to Mar del Plata to start the 2012 Dakar.

The team's staging area was a large warehouse at the back of the main depot for the Tamarugal trucking company near Santiago. It was a spacious, tall building with loads of room to house the two supply transport trucks, the two race cars, and the four bikes, as well as all the parts, bits, and pieces that would be carried with us. Whenever I turned up, I would try to help out where I could, but there really was not much for me to do. Everyone had their roles well defined, their jobs predetermined, and each person went about their business with focus and determination.

This focus is necessary, because preparing for a Dakar Rally is like getting ready to go to war. Competitors and their crews are on their own for fourteen days of racing in very challenging conditions, nowhere near any civilization, and they must think of anything and everything that possibly could go awry. Spare parts, tools, tires, and fluids must be gathered and available at any time or location for each competition vehicle, as well as clothing, tents, mattresses, and other items to keep everyone as comfortable as possible in the bivouacs. Estimates of how much of each item necessary to complete the Dakar must be made, as there is only so much room in the assistance trucks, and superfluous material only gets in the way of what really might be needed.

Will a drive shaft break? Will it happen twice? How many tires will a motorcycle need to complete the Rally? Will oxygen be needed to cross the high mountain passes? How do the competitors manage temperatures that can range from a high of 50°C to a low of −10°? What does each competition vehicle carry with it, as they are not permitted to accept outside help during a race? An incorrect calculation of the right number of a specific part can be catastrophic.

One of the Rally favorites, and the winner of the 2011 Dakar in the car category, Nasser Al-Attiyah from Abu Dhabi, was forced to retire early from the 2012 Rally because he broke three fan belts during a tough ride in the desert, but he only carried two spares with him. For the lack of a $5 fan belt, one of the world's top Rally competitors was forced to withdraw. How frustrating is that? All of these questions, and thousands more, are discussed over many months of preparation as the boxes and boxes of tools and equipment are inspected and loaded for the Rally.

Experience counts, and it is the Dakar veterans who provide the most valuable advice in getting ready for the Rally. The majority of teams begin preparing for the next Dakar immediately following the Rally, with some of the race vehicles taking a year or more to build and provision for the coming event.

The Tamarugal team had spent months preparing for the 2012 Dakar. Many of the drivers, *moto* pilots, and mechanics had been involved in many Rally Raids and the Dakar since it came to South America, and were utilizing this experience to get ready. As I watched and assisted where I could, long lines of plastic boxes were carefully filled with parts and supplies and then labeled to ensure nothing was forgotten. Lists were prepared, reviewed, and then reviewed again. Nothing could be left to chance, everything had to be right, and getting all of this properly organized was a massive logistical undertaking.

The two Tamarugal Rally cars had been built and designed to the exacting specifications of Alejandro Briones, the head of the team and a highly experienced Rally driver. A company specializing in Rally Raid vehicles, Wicked Creations, located in Orange County, California, had constructed the two cars over the prior year.

Calling these custom-fabricated race vehicles "cars" is like referring to a jet fighter as a small, single-engine airplane. The frames, based on a Honda truck body, are composed of welded high-strength aluminum designed for both low weight and strength, the protection of the engine and drive components, as well as the driver and co-driver. The engines, fueled by gasoline or turbo-diesel, generate in excess of four hundred horsepower. The vehicles each weigh only two thousand pounds and are covered with carbon fiber panels painted the distinct Tamarugal yellow, fully festooned with sponsors' logos.

When I first climbed into the driver's compartment of one of our Dakar Rally cars, I realized very quickly that I was not sitting in a standard 4WD vehicle. It was like nothing I had seen before. There were mysterious wires, cables, levers, dials, and gauges everywhere, as well as fire extinguishers, various tools, water delivery systems for driver and navigator, harnesses, special race-designed seats with everything else padded for protection, TV monitors, the Dakar-specified guidance and safety systems, three or four odometers, map holders, wide mesh on the side windows, numerous floor pedals in addition to the accelerator, clutch, and brake, as well as millions of buttons and toggle switches with such esoteric names as "inflation system," "vent off/on," "fuel suppression," "pump off," or "pump manual." On one dashboard I saw during the Rally there was even a set of toggles labeled "These switches are teasing us. They don't do anything but look racy and cool." Also present were the ubiquitous seat-belt cutter and automotive window-smashing hammer, reminding me once again of the dangers facing a Rally team. It took a long time to get strapped in and hooked up to a Dakar vehicle to get ready to race.

The motorcycles were also customized to a high degree, and for the first time on the 2012 Rally, there were engine and chassis specifications specifically designed to reduce risk and require riders to compete based on their skill and endurance rather than the power of their motorcycles. All bikes approved for the 2012 Dakar had to be standard production machines authorized for use on public roads with the major parts—frame, engine, and swing arm—freely available to the public. The major parts could be modified, with the exception of the engine casing, but must respect an extensive list of technical regulations. All bikes must have engines with a cubic capacity up to and including only 450 cc, in either single or twin cylinders. For the quads, the vehicles must also be available to the general public, and can be 2WD or 4WD, two- or four-stroke engines, and with a capacity up to 900 cc.

The *moto* competitors are allowed to change or repair their engines (the part encased in the main engine casing), but the first time they install a new engine the rider is assessed a fifteen-minute time penalty, the second occurrence is given a forty-five–minute penalty, with the third and any following changes adding two hours each to their time. During the 2012 Dakar, I saw the Rally leaders watching each other very carefully to see who would change an engine first. Once done, they then all followed at the same time to ensure they had the same penalties, but also to have the most powerful and reliable power to compete through the final days of the Rally.

Accompanying our Tamarugal race vehicles were two huge

custom-fabricated Mercedes Benz transport trucks adapted to carry all the parts and supplies for the Rally, as well as the mechanics and support crew. These support trucks, categorized as T-5 vehicles by the Rally organizers, must also meet certain rigorous safety criteria and be designed to take a fair beating. Many of the roads traveled between bivouacs will be rough, and the survival of the support crews and vehicles is critical to finishing a Dakar. A number of teams also build support trucks that are designated T-4. These vehicles are designed to actually drive on the race stages and must meet even higher standards for safety and reliability. The Tamarugal team was not fielding a T-4 truck, and, as things turned out, they most likely wished they had.

As we could not catch any of the day two special because of the impassable roads from the rock slides, we arrived at the San Rafael bivouac in the late afternoon. To my surprise, I saw one of our Tamarugal pickup trucks positioned just inside the bivouac gates, surrounded by yellow tape with large Xs covering the registration numbers. My initial thought was that the team was being featured that day, perhaps with a presentation or some sort of recognition. As I soon learned, the recognition was something quite different.

Apparently the team driver, racing to get to the bivouac, had ignored his Tripy bleepings and been clocked by race organizers at over 170 kilometers per hour on the highway. To set an example, and to reinforce the ASO's commitment to adhering to local regulations, our truck had been singled out, impounded, and displayed for all to see. It would not be released until a hefty fine had been paid, and only after the finish of the next day's special. The driver was quite sheepish, but at least the team had not been assessed any time penalties. If it had been a competitor found to be speeding, serious time penalties would have been assessed, as well as significant cash fines that must be paid before being allowed to start the next day's stage. If a race vehicle had been caught at seventy kilometers per hour over the speed limit, the penalty would have been almost three hours added to the driver's overall time, certainly placing him out of contention.

As the San Rafael bivouac was not too busy when we arrived, I ran to the shower rooms. In my almost sixty years I had not been so excited about running water and soap, even if it was cold water, soap out of a dispenser, and an environment characterized by the European tendency for men to ignore they were naked and standing too close to you for comfort. But I was able to get clean, with days of dust washed away. I returned to the Tamarugal compound, and, as I chatted with the guys, my eyes started to close. I remembered the advice from Rick, the mechanic, who had worked on three Dakar Rallies, to grab sleep whenever you could. Secure in my knowledge that I was so tired I would not move an inch to place me in danger, I set up a mattress under one of the supply trucks and lay down. I was fast asleep in about thirty seconds.

While the *moto* side of the Tamarugal compound in the San Rafael bivouac was busily working, the car section was looking very anxious. One car had already blown an engine on day one. Reports were now coming in that the second car was having transmission problems and was stuck in the middle of the stage route. I had dinner with the car mechanics and listened to them discuss how they would prepare for their car's arrival, how long certain repair tasks would take, and what spare parts they would need. When I went to bed about midnight, they were still waiting for the race car to arrive with spare parts and tools all ready and laid out in preparation.

Waking up the next morning brought worse news. The remaining Tamarugal car was still stuck in the dunes from the previous day's stage, and the entire car crew was returning to Santiago. They first had to find a flatbed and rescue both the cars and then drive them back to Chile. There was some talk of the team rejoining us in Copiapó, and I hoped it worked out for them. Their departure placed additional pressure on the *moto* team to perform well for the sponsors, but as they talked with me, it was clear they accepted the challenge willingly and looked forward to being the sole representatives of the Tamarugal name for the rest of the 2012 Dakar. Daniel, in particular, looked even more committed to doing well—a lot was riding on his shoulders, and he knew it.

The only silver lining from this difficult situation was that I would get a properly functioning tent from one of the departing team members. I realized this was awfully selfish, and small comfort for losing our two high-profile race cars to the desert, but it was a blessing nevertheless.

The drive north from San Rafael to the next bivouac in San Juan was spectacular, with the Andes Mountains running beside us to our west.

We knew the race was being held in the foothills, and quite often we could see long lines of *polvo* on our left kicked up by the race vehicles as we drove toward one of the designated spectator areas.

Day three was quite a change from the first two special stages and a very challenging route for the Dakar competitors. After a 291-kilometer liaison from San Rafael, the special started near Uspallata in the foothills of the Andes, close to Mendoza, a region famous for its wine production and the primary source of Malbec, a varietal that has put Argentina prominently on the wine connoisseur's map. The special extended for 270 kilometers over dirt and stone track across numerous riverbeds, some with water and some dry, finishing at the San Juan bivouac. It was a grueling day, as the rough and rocky terrain tested the durability of the race vehicles, with a large number of both *motos* and autos having to retire because of mechanical failure. There were also many steep climbs up and down the cordillera, one in particular forcing vehicles to grind over 1,200 meters steeply up a mountain in first gear, only to find they had to find their way down the other side in an equally steep and treacherous descent. It was also another exceedingly hot day with not a cloud in the sky.

Before climbing into my new tent in San Juan, I noticed a lot of work around Daniel's motorcycle. The brackets holding the Roadbook, Tripy, the odometers, warning devices, and other important navigation and safety equipment on his *moto* had cracked. Daniel felt the bracket was too high, resulting in too much vibration. His mechanic, Chelo, who thought of everything, had another, shorter mounting bracket in the support truck, and through the evening he made the necessary retrofits. Daniel liked the position better, and given the amount of time he spent looking at these devices while riding fast over insanely uneven and tricky terrain, position was everything.

In addition to the supplied Tripy and Roadbook, every competition vehicle must also have on board a number of safety devices sanctioned and supplied by the ASO race organizers. The Sentinel is an important safety device that warns of the proximity of another vehicle. Within the massive dust clouds created by race vehicles, it is almost impossible to know if you are being overtaken, and dire consequences can result if, for example, a slower motorcycle moves the wrong way into the path of a much faster and much heavier car or truck. The Sentinel is triggered by the vehicle wishing to pass, sounding a buzzer and illuminating a light in any vehicle being overtaken within a 150-meter range. The slower vehicle, if it's a car or truck, then acknowledges the signal, sounding a buzzer and illuminating a green light in the passing vehicle, telling the faster driver it is okay to proceed. The *moto* riders do not have to acknowledge the Sentinel signal; they just have to be aware someone is coming. The Sentinel is also used to warn all competitors if they are within five hundred meters of an accident site.

Some less scrupulous competitors use the Sentinel as a tool to advance their positions during the Rally. In one instance described to me by a driver in the car category, he was approaching the back of another car at a time when everyone's vision was obscured by the clouds of *polvo* being thrown up by all the traffic. It was a fairly narrow track within a riverbed, and the faster vehicle, not seeing much room to pass the slower vehicle, signaled his intention using his Sentinel. The driver in front returned the signal and indicated with his right turn flasher that he should be passed on that side of his vehicle. However, as the faster car moved up on the slower car's right side, the driver in front swerved over, forcing the passing car into the riverbed, where he flattened two tires and completely ruined a wheel rim. It took a good forty minutes to change the tires and, with no spares remaining (most cars can carry only two wheel replacements during any given stage), he had to exercise extreme care through the rest of the stage that he did not cause another flat, as he would have been eliminated from the Rally, stuck in the middle of nowhere.

"I thought of trying to find the guy in the bivouac and give him a piece of my mind, but he probably didn't think he had done anything wrong. It's not my style—to win at any cost—but I guess that's how many get ahead in the dog-eat-dog world of the Dakar," the wronged competitor told me.

Daniel had a small fall in the sand on day three, finishing in twenty-seventh position, but because there were a number of riders ahead of him who got lost and missed a waypoint, he moved up to fifteenth in the overall standings. Again, navigation is as important as speed in the Dakar Rally. All of the Tamarugal *moto* riders were tired, dirty, and exhausted. Turning their bikes over to their mechanics on their arrival, they headed off to the showers, sat down for a quick dinner, and then devoted a good hour or two to study the next day's route. They were crawling into their tents around nine, as early the next morning they would face a very challenging special on day four.

CHAPTER SIX
THE PERILS OF DRIVING IN SOUTH AMERICA

The bivouac in San Juan, Argentina, was located on a racetrack nestled between two huge cliffs. With the sun beating relentlessly down on the track surface where we were to camp, the temperature had to be much higher than the forty-one degrees registered on the truck thermometer. Pedro, Rodrigo, and I decided to head into town to find an air-conditioned bar or café where we could access the Internet and cool off with a beer. Rodrigo was pretty good at this espionage. We drove slowly past likely-looking establishments, and if he could see a Wi-Fi site with his mobile phone, we stopped. The problem was, although the Café Freud's router was sending a signal, perhaps like its namesake Sigmund, it was not connected to the outside world. Nevertheless, I had one of the best-tasting beers I had ever had, and we made an executive decision to find a hotel for the night. The option of camping out on a sloping cinder race car track, baking in that high heat, made the decision easy.

After a few tries (all the big hotels were full with Dakar fans), we found a nice little "apart-hotel" farther out at the edge of the city, with a pool and restaurant. We took two rooms but unfortunately were told the pool was temporarily not available.

"A local advertising agency is shooting pictures of female models in bathing suits for a local fashion store," the manager explained. We could watch if we wanted, he said. I opted for a long shower and a nap—that's how dirty and tired you get on the Dakar Rally.

Following a great sleep, a wonderful hot shower where I was blessed with not having to change in close proximity to large naked hairy European men, and then a real hot breakfast, we were on our way by 6:00 a.m., heading to the start area for that day's stage. Day four of the

Dakar began with a long liaison drive of about 350 kilometers to the start of the 326-kilometer special just inside the Parque Nacional San Guillermo.

We wanted to see how the Dakar began the specials each day, and we drove to the marshaling area at a location north of the town of San José de Jáchal. We entered the staging area close to a highway and moved through the security perimeter to get closer to the action. The Dakar organization had the departure from the bivouac and the start of each timed stage perfectly organized. For example, the *motos* and quads had departed the bivouac that morning beginning at 5:30 a.m., and they were scheduled to begin the stage in a defined order starting at 9:45, leaving them plenty of time to ride the liaison stage from the bivouac to the start area. The autos departed the bivouac at 7:16 (not 7:15—I love the extra minute the ASO uses) and began the race at 11:31, while the big trucks rolled out of San Rafael at 9:33 for the race stage at 1:58 p.m. In case there were any mechanical issues, you could still participate in that day's stage as long as you were out of the bivouac by 10:22 a.m. and through the start area by 2:47 p.m. Quite often participants who had been out on the course all night due to being lost or a breakdown took this time in the bivouac to rest and prepare for that day's stage, as we would see later that evening. For most it was enough to just finish all fourteen stages of the Dakar Rally.

We watched as each of our four *motos* drove over to a refueling depot to top up. The gasoline and diesel fuel, preordered and paid for during the registration process back in Mar del Plata, was contained in a large number of steel drums under an awning, pumped by hand into the vehicle tanks by representatives of the ASO's fuel supplier, Total. After filling up, the drivers moved into a compound shaded by large tents, where they could get ready and load up with water to await departure.

The top ten participants from the prior day then rolled up to the start line, and each raced off in two-minute intervals. As we saw during the first special along the Atlantic Coast, the two-minute separation is very important, as it allows the massive amount of *polvo* thrown up by each vehicle to settle and permits much better vision. Each participant is timed separately; it is not a race against others on that day's course, except to post a faster time. The second ten competitors then left one minute apart, Daniel included, the next ten separated by thirty seconds, with the rest setting off in pairs every fifteen seconds. As you can imagine, if you are near the back, you ingest a lot of dust. All vehicles must depart the start area by 2:47 p.m. in order to have the stage count.

Before starting, each rider is first checked off a list by the official starter and given his route ticket for the day. These tickets must be marked at each consecutive checkpoint along the route. They then roll up to the start line, revving their engines, where they are counted down for five seconds by the starter with a hand signal. It's really much too loud for any verbal instructions to be given.

During the stage, the competitors have to pass through a number of designated checkpoints, using their Roadbooks and odometer systems to find them. And they can be missed, as happened on yesterday's stage. Often this is not a major problem—you just turn around when your Tripy or Roadbook warns you, and go back to find the checkpoint. The problem yesterday arose when, after missing the checkpoint, the riders entered a river canyon so narrow that they could not return against oncoming race traffic to correct their error. It took a long detour through the canyon and then back to the checkpoint, adding almost forty minutes to their total time. Luckily Daniel had been in one of the groups that had been checked off as visiting this illusive checkpoint station.

Once Daniel had left the start area, the rest of the Tamarugal riders were on their way, and we watched a few of the car leaders roar out, we headed north to find the spectator area at the finish line somewhere outside Villa Unión, about one hundred kilometers southwest of our next bivouac in Chilecito.

It was another beautiful drive through western Argentina, with the very red cliffs of La Rioja Province as landmarks to remember. The red and ochre colors of the landscape were astonishing, especially in stark contrast to the dark grays and blacks of the Andes Mountains overshadowing them to the west. I was told the red coloring is due to the high copper and iron mineral content close to the surface throughout the region, and I was sure the views would gain the attention of all the competitors as they raced along through the narrow canyons and dry riverbeds of dirt and gravel track on today's route, their speed being cautioned by large boulders, close rock faces, and sharp turns. In the briefing the night before, the ASO warned competitors that navigation skills would be seriously tested toward the end of the special near the Chilecito bivouac, and a number of riders did get lost. All through that evening and into the early morning hours we could hear vehicles arriving in the dark, their pilots frustrated at having spent so much time trying to find their way.

As we drove north that day toward the spectator area near Chilecito, we often saw plumes of *polvo* to our west, marking the path of the Dakar competitors. I'll be quite happy if I don't see *polvo* again for many years. It gets into everything, and I now know why the Dakar logo depicts a person with their head wrapped in one of those large scarves. I wish I had one.

By now we were old and experienced hands at finding the designated spectator zones using GPS coordinates to guide us to the locations. The ASO, in discussion with local police forces, tries to pick areas where as many people as possible can safely obtain a good view of the vehicles racing by. Typically they are in the middle of nowhere, and no services are offered. Still, thousands of fans turn up at these designated areas to spend the day watching the Dakar. They bring their own food and drink, awnings for shade, chairs, family and friends, and everything else needed for a long day in the county. Many cook their lunch and dinner over open fires. It's a busy place, made more hectic by the South American tendency to push the crowd envelope and try to get as close as possible to the action. Despite the best efforts of the police and organization staff, spectators are killed every year as they try to get that perfect picture.

And then there are the dogs. There are a lot of dogs in South America. Most families own two or three, especially in the countryside, where they act as companions and an inexpensive and highly effective security system. These animals are generally not tied up or confined in any way, and they are free to roam around, looking for fun and frolic, returning home for meals and sleep during the hot sun of the day.

Adding to the numbers of pet dogs is the vast quantity of *quiltros*, dogs abandoned by their owners. Typically what happens is the cute little puppy the kids brought home grows into a 100-pound behemoth with huge teeth and a slobbering problem. One night Dad takes Rover out into the countryside and returns home with a hopeful story about how their dear pet has gone to live on a farm or with a shepherd. In reality, Dad has simply left Rover at the side of some quiet country road and driven away.

You see these *quiltros* everywhere in South America. The cities and towns are full of them—everything from large breeds such as German shepherds down to the smallest spaniels and beagles, as well as everything in between, as they tend to breed indiscriminately. It is estimated that in Santiago, Chile, alone there are some two hundred thousand *quiltros* roaming the streets. Restaurants are a destination of choice, as most families take their meals outside and the *quiltros*, understanding politeness and manners, wait for handouts or sympathetic restaurant owners to feed them.

The roads near our Chilean home are a popular area for residents of Santiago to increase the *quilltro* population. In addition to kind souls who leave large sacks of dog food on the side of the roads for the *quiltros* to eat, others visit local restaurants and butchers to obtain surplus bones and meat, leaving this welcome source of nourishment for their well-being. During one of my first bicycle rides after moving into our house, I was quite alarmed when I came across a pack of these large, unkempt, and wild-looking dogs gnawing on bloody chunks of meat and bone. Fearing these might have been the remains of the last cyclist who had the misfortune to run this gauntlet, I beat a measured but hasty retreat. I learned later that it is very rare for these dogs to harm anyone, and they are all very friendly. If you stop near where the *quiltros* are resting, they will jump up, tails wagging, and gather around you, hoping against hope that you might take one home with you. They will lick your hands and try to climb in your vehicle. It is very, very sad to see their disappointed faces as you leave them behind.

Because the dog population in South America is so large, the practice of veterinary medicine has become quite widespread and lucrative. Vets will come to your home to treat your pets, bringing with them any shots, pills, or surgical equipment that might be required. They will also take your dog away for serious work, returning the pet once it has fully recovered. You can't get this type of home visit from a doctor, but for your dog anything goes.

And the *quiltros* seem to be a lot smarter than Dakar spectators, as you see very few of the stray dogs wandering onto the racecourse, thank goodness.

The spectator area we visited near the Chilecito bivouac was well situated and an excellent example of how well this event was organized. There was a long straight stretch of track in a partially dry riverbed that took competitors toward the crowd positioned on a number of hills surrounding the special route. The pilots then slowed for a hard left turn in front of the fans, accelerating away from the spectator area along another riverbed. It was a great vantage point, but the temperature was over forty degrees, with mountains of dry *polvo* being whipped up by high winds and the passing *motos* and cars. While the crowds had their Argentinian favorites, the cheers were loud and enthusiastic for every participant.

First through were the elite *moto* riders, and were they ever fast. You could tell these experienced leaders were riding right on the edge of disaster, but that is what it takes to win a Dakar. By comparison to the less experienced riders, the difference was quite noticeable. Once the elite riders were through, Daniel included, little packs of riders arrived, sometimes accompanied by one of the better quad riders who had started after the *motos* and caught up to them.

I really wanted to see the cars in action, and I was not disappointed. The first to appear was Nasser Al-Attiyah, the winner of last year's Dakar for Volkswagen, but this year running a big and powerful gray-colored Hummer. He stole the show. Following Nasser was one of the Minis, a new brand to the Dakar this year and one many believed would be tough to beat. Then came Robby Gordon, the US-based NASCAR driver, in his bright-orange Hummer, followed by another Mini and then a Toyota. By this point the slower bikes and quads were being passed by the elite car drivers, and it was a bit chaotic in the dust and the water of the river. That was the thrill of the Dakar.

One reason the cars can run so much faster is that the navigator passes direction and road condition instructions to the driver over a communication system. It is the navigator's job to know, understand,

and follow each day's Roadbook, while the driver simply goes as fast as he can with the given verbal instructions, confident they are being informed about everything that is ahead. The cars also have the advantage of using their Sentinel systems to warn slower vehicles they want to pass. The *moto* riders, on the other hand, have to do both jobs—drive fast *and* follow their Roadbook. You can see them looking down frequently to see what is coming, and a couple of the more inexperienced riders at the spectator area we were watching locked up their wheels and swung wide on the turn, as clearly they were not sure what was around the next corner. Riding a *moto* in the Dakar takes skill, patience, nerve, and a lot of calm. I continued to be so impressed by Daniel and the rest of the *moto* competitors.

Following the Dakar can be a bit of a science. The exact locations of these spectator areas, like the one where we spent most of the day, are not announced until two days before each stage, and are indicated with GPS coordinates along with a rough reference on maps to nearby towns. Somehow thousands of spectators find their way to spend the day watching the Dakar.

But they also all have to go home, and combined with the many competitors and assistance vehicles following the liaison route heading to the next bivouac, there can be a lot of traffic. The crowds of vehicles driving to the Chilecito bivouac created some interesting situations. At one point the pavement ended and we found ourselves on a narrow dirt road (more *polvo!*) winding steeply up and then down through a serious set of mountains and valleys.

Behind the wheel of our truck, my mind constantly wandered to all the news reports I had read about buses and cars plunging over cliffs, killing everyone aboard. I remembered that vehicle maintenance was less than stellar in the developing countries of South America. In North America, we have become accustomed to safe roads and well-enforced rules, the result of billions of dollars of tax revenue spent annually on infrastructure and well-paid police forces dedicated to saving lives, if not simply meeting revenue quotas with traffic tickets. Our vehicles at home are also well maintained, generally modern, with excellent brake, suspension, and safety systems. But in South America, it is a world of difference. Here, infrastructure funding is scarce, vehicles are maintained on shoestring budgets, if at all, and the underpaid police are often bribed to look the other way.

In May 2011, the World Health Organization launched its "Decade of Action for Road Safety," citing statistics that showed traffic accidents were rapidly becoming one of the leading causes of preventable death around the world. Approximately 1.2 million people are killed in traffic accidents each year, or almost three thousand people each and every day. Even more worrying, the countries the Dakar was visiting this year were quite high in the statistics of traffic-related deaths, with Peru topping the list at 391 fatalities annually per 100,000 vehicles in service. Compare this statistic to only 7 per 100,000 vehicles in the United Kingdom, thirteen in Canada, and fifteen in the United States, and you can understand my concern as I desperately fought to avoid plunging over the cliffs beside me.

The drive north, under normal conditions, would have been breathtaking; however, with the hundreds of Dakar vehicles heading north, many of them race vehicles designed for this type of terrain and driven by professionals skilled at these conditions and anxious to get to the bivouac for food, rest, and repairs, it was a very scary drive. The road was really narrow, and there were few barriers or walls to stop you from heading over some very steep and deep cliffs. At the same time, race *motos*, quads, and cars were trying to pass whenever they could, all throwing up choking dust clouds that made visibility almost impossible. I was driving, and it was no fun.

The only solution I could find was to stick as close as possible to the car in front and hope they could see where they were going. And compounding the dangers of the drive were the spectators lined up to say hello, standing in and around many of the sharper corners, all positioned close to the road and occasionally darting into traffic for a picture or to shake a hand. Fortunately, it all ended well, but at times I was wondering if an *animita* would have to be erected in my memory and who would give my eulogy.

Arriving at the Chilecito bivouac, I wandered into the Red Bull hospitality tent and found myself seated beside Camélia Liparoti, one of the few women competing in this year's Dakar and currently standing tenth overall in the quad category. Camélia's two-man support crew and vehicle had not yet arrived at the bivouac, and it was too early to obtain and study the next day's Roadbook, so she had some time to chat with me.

Of French and Italian parents, Camélia is a petite blonde, her hair tied up in her trademark pigtails, with a winning smile and an air of complete confidence. She is friendly and charming, and with her signature pink helmet, she attracted a lot of attention during her previous three attempts at completing the Dakar.

She came to quad racing by a rather circuitous route. Now in her early forties (she would not tell me how old she was, admitting only that she "was just the right age"), she had started out as a world-class extreme skier in Switzerland, using jobs as a photographer during the off-season to pay the bills. In 2005, she was sent by a sponsoring sunglass company to photograph and cover the Dakar in Northeast Africa, where the company provided her with a quad to travel out to the sand dunes of the racecourse.

As she rode her quad in the dunes, she recognized how close the driving of a quad was to her sport of extreme skiing. "It was the sliding down steep slopes, the similar terrain, the sand feeling a lot like snow, and the same skills necessary to go fast and stay upright. I was hooked," she told me. And she has been very successful. Three-time winner of the World All-Terrain Rally Cup in the women's moto-quad category, she had targeted a top-ten finish for her fourth Dakar Rally.

Another competitor in the car category used the same analogy to describe navigating the dunes: "Driving in the sand dunes is a real experience. It's like snowboarding," he told me. "When you get it right, it flows so beautifully, it's like looking at a big bowl of powder snow that no one has been in. In your mind you can see that you should bank around that rock, slide towards those trees, keep up the momentum. But when you get it wrong, it's like drowning. You can't get enough momentum to climb, you're forcing your engine, the axles are shaking, everything is getting hot, you're getting nervous that you're going to get stuck. You need to understand how the wind shapes things in the dunes, which side is hard enough to hold a car and which is too soft. You need to know what your car can, and can't, do. It's definitely a skill you have to learn, and I am still learning," he admitted.

But why did Camélia compete in such a dangerous activity? "I do it for my friends and my family," she told me. "We all live for adventure, it's a passion within us, and the Dakar is the ultimate test." I hope she achieves her dream.

Daniel came twenty-fourth in stage four, moving down a bit in the overall standings to seventeenth position. He told me that he recognized today's route could be dangerous and he did not want to push himself too much in the heat and dust. Hopefully it was the right decision. And there were quite a few crashes, in both the *moto* and car categories, with a few participants needing medical attention, while a number got lost during the difficult navigation challenges presented toward the end of the special. I noticed a lot of bandages and splints in the dining area that night. The first goal of Dakar participation is to *finish* the Rally, and I believe Daniel demonstrated a lot of maturity in his decisions to take it a bit easier that day.

CHAPTER SEVEN
CROSSING THE ANDES: FROM +40°C TO -5°C IN ONE DAY

Day five of the 2012 Dakar was interesting on a number of fronts. The *moto* guys got up quite early, as they were normally scheduled to leave the bivouac around 5:00 a.m. Thus, their alarms started ringing about 4:00, and as I had spent the night in my new tent close to the group as protection from last night's dust storm, I was up early with them. I had the luxury of time to take a shower (cold again), have a Dakar breakfast (croissants, coffee, odd-looking omelets, and juice), and wander around watching competitors and their mechanics get ready and break camp as the sun rose over the mountains. Many teams had two large transport trucks, sending one on to the next bivouac early to get a good position, while the second stayed behind for any last-minute mechanical problems before departure or during the liaison. With the retirement of our entire car crew on day two, we were reduced to one supply vehicle and had to make sure we used it judiciously, sending it out immediately after everyone departed to ensure it would be ready and waiting at the next bivouac for the arrival of our *motos*.

Once everyone was up and ready, we hurried to the bivouac gate, only to be one of the vehicles randomly selected each day to be "breathalized" for alcohol. At 6:00 a.m., Pedro received a perfect "000," probably the only test where getting zero is the best score.

Today's race comprised two separate specials, one for the *motos* and a second, different stage for the autos and trucks closer to the next bivouac in Fiambalá. The routes were divided as a result of a number of problems that occurred in the deep and heavy sand dunes in this region during the previous year's Dakar. While the autos and trucks were able, with some difficulty, to navigate through the sand, the *motos* last year had a particularly challenging time, with a large number becoming bogged down and requiring rescue. To avoid this problem, the *motos* and quads ran a different special stage that took them north in a 265-kilometer arc away from the dunes captured by the mountain valley, bordered by the Cerro Morado to the north, the Cordillera de San Buenaventura to the west, and the Cordillera de los Andes to the south. To compensate for the reduced challenge of managing the sand dunes, the ASO had plotted some very difficult navigational trials into the *moto* and quad special that would become readily apparent early in the race. The autos and trucks would run a 177-kilometer loop taking them farther into the sand and dunes of the valley than the prior year's disastrous route. All classes finished their respective specials descending a huge sand mountain directly beside the Fiambalá bivouac.

We drove as quickly as possible along the 151-kilometer liaison route, mindful of our cursed Tripy and its obnoxious speed warnings, to spend the afternoon at a checkpoint where competitors had their route tickets marked to ensure they were on the right track and following the prescribed special. The times at each checkpoint were also sent to the Rally organizers by satellite and published on the Dakar website in real time to allow fans and the media to get a sense of how their favorite competitors were performing that day.

On each race vehicle, as part of the proprietary ASO GPS device, a locator signal appeared when a pilot was approximately two hundred meters from a scheduled checkpoint, and then turned off once the competitor had registered and moved on. This feature proved very helpful today.

The checkpoint was at the end of a long and narrow dirt track crossing a main road near Londres, Argentina. Once checked in, the riders were supposed to traverse the road, with all traffic being stopped by local police, and then make a sharp left turn onto another long straight dirt track heading north and west. It looked like the ideal place to watch the action, and I remained at the waypoint while Rodrigo and Pedro walked down the track to get pictures.

The first *moto* pilot through the checkpoint was Marc Coma, the overall leader in the *moto* category. He properly came down the dirt track, had his card stamped, and charged off. Everything was done quickly and efficiently.

But less than two minutes later, Cyril Despres, running in second place in the *moto* group, came to the checkpoint from a completely different direction, riding down the paved road nowhere near the dirt track. He looked confused, talked briefly to the stewards, who pointed behind him, and then took off in pursuit of Coma. The race officials looked concerned, including Etienne Lavigne, the head of ASO, who had arrived by helicopter to watch the stage.

I spoke with Lavigne, who told me the navigation on this stage had been planned to be particularly difficult, and to back this up we could hear *motos* starting and stopping in the woods all around the checkpoint. Most were coming down the road the way Despres had come, likely following his and the tracks of others. It is standard practice, when lost, to see where those ahead of you have gone, hoping they are heading in the right direction. However, this must have been a very challenging orienteering exercise, as riders were appearing from all directions, including from the woods near the checkpoint, scattering the spectators and sending police running. Clearly almost everyone was lost, but when their GPS systems kicked in, showing them the direction to the checkpoint, they just rode toward it. It was quite exciting, and the spectators were enthralled. It was also interesting to see the riders adjusting their navigation systems and resetting their odometers to agree with the location of the waypoint, critical in their ability to navigate through to the next checkpoint on the stage.

As we were driving toward Fiambalá once the majority of *motos* had checked in, Pedro, Rodrigo, and I discussed plans for the next few days. Tomorrow was the scheduled mass crossing of the border into Chile through the Paso San Francisco, the highest road on the continent at over 4,700 meters, or more than 15,500 feet above sea level. Customs formalities for both countries were being completed in the Fiambalá bivouac, but with a special scheduled for later that day, and the *motos* to leave the bivouac at 4:00 a.m., it would be a very early departure, with most likely long lines and waiting at both border crossings. We also understood that the assistance vehicles, us included, would be held in the bivouac until all the race vehicles had departed. It would be a long and frustrating day, and we decided to check in that afternoon, clear customs at the bivouac, and then drive over the pass to Copiapó for the night ahead of the crush the following morning.

Another of the reasons we wanted to attempt the border crossing on our own was our memory of what we encountered at the crossing into Argentina when we brought the team from Santiago to Mar del Plata for the registration and organization days before the Rally began.

We had departed from the team's headquarters in Lampa, just north of Santiago, on December 27, giving us three days for the almost 1,500-kilometer drive east across Argentina to Buenos Aires and then south to Mar del Plata. Immediately on leaving the Santiago region, we headed north to Los Andes and then east into the Andes Mountains, climbing steeply through more than fifty tight and narrow switchbacks to the fabled ski resort of Portillo, overlooked by Mount Aconcagua, at almost seven thousand meters above sea level, the highest mountain in South America. It was an astonishingly beautiful drive, with the mountains changing color frequently from a dark gray and black, through various shades of red, gold, and copper under massive, craggy snowcapped peaks, and ending finally in the lush and deep greens of the vineyards of Mendoza, Argentina, on the easternmost side of the Andes. Despite the stunning vistas and bold colors, you did need to pay attention at all times, as the road was narrow and steep, the turns sharp, and as this highway was the main commercial route between Chile and Argentina, there were large numbers of transport trucks and tourist buses both ascending and descending. It could get quite dangerous.

At the route's summit, we faced the first challenge of our 2012 Dakar, the agonizing process of going through the various customs procedures. The crossing into Argentina is famous for taking forever. The first time I crossed through the border at the Paseo Cristo Redentor, it took almost five hours with only a small vehicle and one friend. I remember thinking, *Boy, we sure don't take this long at home to go through a border check,* and then, once again, recalled my lawyer's wise advice.

Part of the issue faced by travelers moving between Chile and Argentine is the long-held animosity felt by citizens of one country for the other. There are no real defining moments for why this ill will is maintained—there have been few wars or skirmishes between the two countries—but the enmity exists, and it is palpable. Chileans think their neighbors are arrogant, with little to be arrogant about; they talk too much, mostly about themselves; and Argentinians cheat at the game of football. Argentinians believe their western neighbors are a bit dim, boring, short, and unattractive, and that Chileans also cheat when playing the national pastime of football. Whatever the reason for the strong feelings within the two countries, the lack of respect extends into the border crossings, and one can be delayed for long periods of time for no apparent reason other than one country trying to irritate the other.

This time at the border there were seven trucks loaded with parts, motorcycles, 4WD cars, fluids, and a mass of other supplies attempting to get through, all manned by guys in bright yellow T-shirts and black pants covered in corporate logos. If it had taken five hours to clear one vehicle my last time through, I wondered how long it would take to move this convoy into Argentina. Fortunately, for the most part, the border officiating went quite smoothly until customs learned we had oil. Apparently there was an oil tax, with the amount subject to negotiation.

"That will be 1,500 pesos for the fuel tax," the Argentinian customs agent told us. "No, make it 1,000 pesos. No, it's 1,500 pesos. That's the correct amount. I think." There were no reference charts or tables, and we were sure it was an arbitrary amount. But we paid, and we were on our way in a remarkable two hours. The 1,500 pesos was about three US dollars.

Another factor in our decision to leave Fiambalá early to cross back into Chile was hearing that there may be weather issues in the mountains. At 4,700 meters, any inclement weather could close the road and the border due to dangerous driving conditions. The air temperature also changed dramatically, in our case falling from a high of 40°C in Fiambalá to below zero at the summit of the pass after only a few short hours of driving. However, the Argentinian police in the Fiambalá bivouac assured us the pass was open, and we left, driving through stunning scenery, the mountains a mix of deep red, gray, and black, and, suddenly and worryingly, the start of some rain.

When we reached the Argentinian border control, the gates were closed, with a handful of Dakar vehicles idling while their drivers heatedly argued with the border guards. Apparently the Chilean

Carabineros had closed their side of the border because of the possibility the rain could turn into snow. Maybe they just wanted to piss off anyone coming from Argentina, but there was no way we could get through. You would think someone would have relayed this information to the Fiambalá bivouac, but this is South America, and they don't do things the way we do at home! We had to either spend the night at the border in the truck, enduring subzero temperatures and rain turning to sleet, or head back to the bivouac in the dark.

Adding to our concerns was the issue of fuel. There were no gasoline stations between Fiambalá and Copiapó, a distance of about 550 kilometers, and while we had filled the tank before we left Fiambalá and carried three large spare gas cans with us, we calculated that we did not have enough fuel to go all the way back to Fiambalá and then drive the return trip to Copiapó. We would have to find fuel with everyone else on the Dakar in Fiambalá, adding to the mess.

About halfway on the drive up to the border, we noticed a strange-looking, elongated concrete building off to one side of the highway, obviously newly built, with a herd of touring motorcycles and a few transport trucks parked in front. On the return trip down from the closed border, we decided to drive in, discovering that the parking lot was now much fuller with vehicles, like us, turned back at the border. It turned out the property was a new hotel, still under construction, and with a bit of haggling we managed to secure the last free room, fortunately with three beds.

But once again, the establishment did not accept credit cards, and as we counted through the small Argentinian peso notes we scrounged from our pockets and throughout the truck, we realized we were short the required amount. We looked around the lobby, and, to our surprise, we saw the same friendly NBC photographers and ASO driver we had met trying to get through the landslides a few days earlier. They loaned us the shortfall of fifty US dollars in cash, and we had just enough to pay for the room. The hotel owners would accept US currency but would not take Chilean notes from their neighbor to the west—another typical example of the strong feelings between the two countries. We had no idea what we would have done if the film crew had not come through for us. The room fee included a basic dinner of beef and pasta, during which the camera crew continued their charity and bought us poor souls each a beer, by which time it was midnight and I could not keep my eyes open.

We also learned from the Dakar officials stranded at the hotel with us that the following day's special stage in Copiapó had been canceled. The organizers did not want to risk sending the *motos* out of the Fiambalá bivouac at 4:00 a.m. to climb the highway into the cold and snow, only to have them stopped at the border. They opted to delay the departure from the bivouac to ensure the border was open and driving conditions were safe. We decided on an early start the next morning, as the entire Dakar bivouac would be headed our way in a very long convoy, and we wanted to beat the rush to the border.

Even when waking and getting ready for a 4:00 a.m. start, the morning rituals to prepare for a Dakar stage become an integral part of a *moto* competitor's life. Just like us normal folk get up on the same side of the bed each morning, wash, brush our teeth, and put our clothes on (pants first, one leg at a time!) in the same order, it is staggering to think how much can be forgotten when preparing to head out to race a motorcycle on a Dakar stage. I had spent a few days watching as each Tamarugal *moto* team member emerged from their tent and then got ready to head out to the start area. Their minds and their gazes were fixed on the route and the stage ahead, while their bodies seemed to automatically go through specific rituals to prepare.

First they dress, and there is a lot to put on. For a Canadian, it is like seeing hockey players don equipment. Specialized undergarments are worn, with chamois sections to protect certain, more tender areas of the male anatomy that can encounter much stress from the narrow and lightly padded motorcycle seat. Kevlar knee and chin guards are strapped on. Pants with thigh protection, liberally covered with sponsors' logos, are then pulled over. Heavy, knee-high leather and plastic boots are buckled on. A layer of upper body protection is worn like a shirt, covering shoulders and arms, with a softer layer of protection for the chest and back. Then much stronger Kevlar chest and back armor is strapped on, with a bladder containing water and electrolytes to fight dehydration placed over the shoulders and attached to the back, with a nozzle running around the neck toward the mouth. Another bladder and nozzle are put on, this containing a protein mix in a milkshake form, as it is tough for *moto* riders to eat while racing on a special. Then the Dakar-approved and mandatory neck brace is buckled on, and finally the jacket is worn, containing about a million necessary pockets, bearing more logos with the all-important Dakar number bib clearly displayed.

The pockets are filled with such things as snacks, road tolls in the correct currency (the Roadbook provides information about how much they need and where—imagine being held up on a liaison stage because you did not have a couple of pesos for a toll!), wet wipes to clean the goggles and different shades of lens should the light change, essential small tools, a rain jacket, a satellite phone, and many other little personal items to help a rider successfully get through the day. Fingers are taped to help avoid blisters, especially on the throttle hand, which cannot be taken off the handlebar for the entire day—there is no such thing as cruise control on a Dakar motorcycle—and light flexible protective gloves are put on. Earplugs are inserted, as the hours of loud engine noise combined with the whistle of wind on and through the helmet can be exhausting. A bandana or head scarf covers the top of the head or around the forehead to control perspiration from dripping into the eyes, and then the special Rally helmet is put on with a long peak over the front to provide some shade from the sun and to protect the face from trees and bushes—the native acacia tree is found everywhere, with millions of sharp pointed spikes growing from its branches. Goggles follow.

Necessary tools are also attached all over the bike, where they can be accessed easily but are not in the way of riding. They carry such items as drive chain master links to fix a broken chain, metal paste to repair any holes or punctures in key parts like an engine casing, spare brake and clutch levers that can be easily broken in a fall, safety wire, zip ties and duct tape to fix other mishaps resulting from a crash, three or four sizes of wrenches and sockets (mechanics will try to standardize all fastenings on a bike to reduce the number of wrench sizes needed), a spark plug tool and spare plugs, vice grips and pliers, screwdrivers, and Allen keys. Competitors are only allowed to receive assistance from other vehicles on the same stage, and with most competitors unwilling to add time by stopping to help another, riders must be prepared to fix almost everything themselves.

All of this must be done each and every morning, and nothing can be omitted. It has to become a ritual for each pilot, so standard and regular that everything is done without thinking. Yet I also saw each rider's mechanic carefully watching to ensure nothing was missed and jumping up to help if a shoulder strap was stuck or a jacket was proving difficult to put on.

Rider preparation was just as important for liaison sections as it was for the race stages, and the drive to Copiapó across the San Francisco Pass was no easy task for the *moto* riders. The temperature would drop from approximately 40°C to −5°C within a matter of hours as the riders climbed the mountain pass. All of them carried oxygen bottles and masks, tucked into the layers of warm clothing they had to wear to get through the day.

When I reached the border crossing at the summit of the pass, I was completely unprepared for the affect the altitude would have on me. My head was pounding with the worst headache I had experienced, and just bending over to tie a shoelace took all the will and stamina I could muster. And while the recently fallen snow from the previous night was beautiful, glistening in the sun, it was damn cold too. When Daniel came through with his thick snowmobile suit and oxygen strapped to his mouth, I was very happy the team had considered every contingency for his safety and success.

The other fascinating thing about Rally racing is that not only must the pilot's body and mind be in perfect working order, in this competitive sport a rider's machine must also be perfect. Thus, there is a long-standing and highly respectful partnership between each rider and their mechanic. The partnership has a language all their own, their communication is more intuitive than direct, and most of the time they can finish each other's sentences. The mechanic knows his rider's motorcycle intimately, and also how his rider wants his bike set up.

The relationship between rider and mechanic is never more important than when something happens out in the field during a stage. Two days ago I watched as Claudio Rodriguez, the fourth rider on the Tamarugal team, arrived at the bivouac following an accident that ripped off one of the engine-cooling radiators on his bike. Each bike has two coolant systems, one on each side of the front structural frame, ensuring a rider can continue should one system fail or, in this case, be torn off. When it happened, Claudio called his mechanic by satellite phone, who, when given a verbal description of the damage, told him to whittle two sticks into a taper and jam one into each of the two coolant hoses from the missing radiator so they would not drain fluids onto the engine. Then he must bind and cover each stick tightly with electrical tape, and fix these now blocked hoses to the frame with cable ties. Claudio was able to finish the stage, although he had lost a lot of time.

Still, the main objective is to *finish* a Rally, and the strong relationship between a rider and mechanic ensured this competitor would continue with his Dakar.

CHAPTER EIGHT
AVOIDING MY "BAD GOOFY"

It was the first stop in Chile for the 2012 Dakar, and at the Copiapó bivouac was the traditional mid-Rally rest day. As helicopters hovered overhead, bringing abandoned *motos* dangling from cables back to the bivouac, the teams got a chance to catch some well-earned sleep and a full day when vehicles can be totally overhauled to prepare for the real test of this year's event—the sand, dunes, and heat of northern Chile and southern Peru. Many people had told me the real Dakar Rally began in Copiapó, and this sobering thought lent a serious sense of urgency to the competitors remaining in the race.

One of the pleasures for competitors and teams alike is the opportunity afforded by the rest day for family and friends to visit the bivouac and catch up, and there was a mass influx of new faces to the Tamarugal compound. Don Omar had brought a group of friends and company VIPs north in his private jet, hosting an *asado* for everyone on the team, complete with wine and beer. It had been some time since any of us had enjoyed a drink stronger then Red Bull, and the supplies disappeared quite quickly.

As the new visitors left for their hotels in town, many of the spouses and significant others remained to spend the two days with their partners, and we organized an informal party, sitting around the trucks talking and drinking well into the night. One lovely young woman had come north to be with her boyfriend, Chelo, Daniel Gouët's mechanic. She spoke English very well, despite her protestations to the contrary, and in a loud voice, becoming louder with each slug of the high-alcohol content Jägermeister she was mixing with her Red Bull, she exhorted me to get drunk.

"Come on, gringo, loosen up, have some fun. *Drink*, gringo, *drink*. Get *drunk*, gringo," she insisted, numerous times, all with a smile and a twinkle in her eyes.

Nearing sixty years of age, getting drunk and sitting around in near 40°C heat under a blazing sun held little allure for me, especially as I contemplated another night of tenting on the hard ground in the swirling *polvo* storms and getting lost trying to find the latrines. A hangover on the Dakar would not be a pretty sight. Still, I joined in, listening to the tinny rock music from an iPod speaker and trying to understand the fast-spoken Spanish all around me.

Despite my reservations, I almost listened to the "Bad Goofy" on my shoulder. You may remember the classic dilemma faced by the Disney character Pluto as he wrestled with his "Good Goofy" on one shoulder, wearing an angel's halo and wings, while his darker counterpart on the opposite shoulder, sporting devil's horns and a trident, encouraged him to be reckless, pay no attention to convention, and live life to its fullest. Everyone needs a "Bad Goofy" in their lives, but this time I turned to the "Good Goofy" in my life and enjoyed the alcohol in moderate quantities.

However, if I had succumbed to the pleas of my "Bad Goofy" and followed my team member's encouragement to get drunk, the next morning I could always visit the nearby medical center set up in the bivouac. While not really there to help with hangovers, the facility was equipped to deal with almost any medical situation or emergency, because the Dakar Rally could be a very dangerous event for both competitors and spectators. More than fifty people have perished in and around the Rally in its thirty-four-year history, with the 2012 edition already seeing one competitor and two spectators die, along with a number of very serious injuries.

Being prepared for such medical emergencies, as well as the normal ailments that can affect a group of over three thousand people—a population larger than most small towns—is a huge task key to the success of the Dakar. Medical staff perform between one hundred and two hundred consultations each day of the Rally, with most of these meetings after 6:00 p.m., when the competitors return to the bivouac following the race, but not until they have first looked after the health and fitness of their vehicles!

ZERO TO SIXTY

Dr. Florence Pommerie is a petite Parisian with short blonde hair, a welcoming smile, and, in conversation with her, a caring and compassionate soul. Dr. Pommerie is the Medical Manager for the Dakar Rally, responsible for a staff of fifty-seven, including emergency room specialists, physiotherapists, surgeons, anesthetists, and ER nurses resident in each day's bivouac. In addition, there are ten emergency vehicles, each staffed with two medical personnel, positioned along the race special routes, and she has access to four helicopters for emergency medical evacuation, again each staffed with an emergency doctor and nurse specialist.

It is important that medical staff are able to respond to questions and situations in all the different languages spoken on the Dakar Rally. This year's group of medical professionals included doctors and other specialists from France, England, Japan, Russia, Peru, Argentina, Chile, and Italy, among others, with many being proficient in two or three different languages. As I waited in the medical center to speak with Dr. Pommerie, I heard four different languages spoken by people coming in for medical assistance, and all were handled in their own language with patience and care.

The method of communicating medical situations on the special routes has been carefully and efficiently designed. Each vehicle competing in the Dakar has an Irritrack system installed and hardwired into their vehicle. During the registration and inspections back at Mar del Plata, the efficacy of these systems was tested to ensure they would function properly in all conditions. Each Irritrack is equipped with a GPS locating system that tells the ASO exactly where every competition vehicle is located at all times, as well as a medical beacon system accessed by three color-coded buttons. The blue button activates an intercom between the vehicle and medical staff in the bivouac. This is used to ask questions should the competitor not feel well or want some noncritical medical information—if used, you will hear a heavily French-accented voice say something like "Eez everysing okay for you?" The yellow button is used primarily when another competitor has come across a medical situation and wants to alert staff as to what has happened. The red button means it is a serious situation and to send help immediately.

When an Irritrack signal is received, a helicopter is readied for takeoff no matter what medical staff might know of a situation. The red signal is also transmitted by satellite to medical staff in Paris, France where officials can coordinate the response with local personnel. For example, it may be faster for one of the on-route medical vehicles to respond to an emergency rather than sending a helicopter. The coordination of the response is done between Paris, the bivouac hospital, and on-route medical vehicles.

The Irritrack is also equipped with sensors that alert medical staff if a vehicle has been stopped for an unusual length of time, there is no response from the competitor, or if the angle of the vehicle has reached a critical point where clearly an accident has occurred. Again, medical staff are alerted and dispatched whenever such a signal is received.

Once medical staff reach an accident site, the situation is assessed and a decision is made to either evacuate the victim to the bivouac medical center or, if available, a local hospital with a helipad. During the previous year's 2011 Dakar Rally, medical staff were able to respond at an average of under twenty minutes following the notification of an accident, an incredible record given the distance and complexity of the race specials and the difficult terrain the competitors traverse.

Within the medical center at each bivouac, the team has the ability to perform both light surgery, such as setting broken bones and dressing abrasions, as well as utilizing a fully equipped intensive care unit (ICU) for more serious cases. I asked Dr. Pommerie about cleanliness and contagion issues that might occur, operating in a tent with a dirt floor and in the middle of the frequent dust storms we encounter.

"This is not really a problem for us," she related. "The real threat is bacteria, and the sand and dirt that make up most of the Dakar Rally environment is relatively benign. In fact, as you can see, our ICU is relatively open to the elements." Looking around at the tent walls being blown around by the ever-present dust storms, I had to trust her experience and expertise.

To assist the medical staff, during registration each competitor is interviewed to get a clear and accurate record of any and all medical conditions, medications being taken, allergies, etc. These histories are important for obvious reasons, but also because the staff is dealing with very fit and highly motivated athletes who are loath to leave the Rally for any medical reason. Medical staff are, thus, able to truly assess a competitor's condition and recommend to Rally officials whether or not someone should be allowed to continue the Rally should a medical situation arise.

Dr. Pommerie told me the story of one *moto* rider who came to the bivouac hospital complaining of a sore wrist. "It was clear the pilot had broken his wrist," she told me. "We asked when the injury had occurred, and were told the accident had happened three days earlier. He had stabilized his wrist by cutting a plastic coke bottle in half and taping it around his injured hand. He thought he could continue if we would only stabilize his wrist a little better." The answer was no, and the rider had to withdraw.

Other common ailments are fatigue and heat issues. Rally participants face dramatically high temperatures, normally between 35°C and 40°C and, in some cases as the Rally moves north, reaching 50°C. Accentuating the heat problems are the layers of protective clothing worn by the competitors that are not conducive to such high temperatures. One situation arose this year during an earlier stage when a *moto* rider became unresponsive because of heat-related issues.

"With a body temperature of over fifty-two degrees, his internal functions were beginning to shut down," Dr. Pommerie explained. "Fortunately our staff reached him on time, managed to stabilize him with ice baths, and get him to a hospital, where he is recovering. If we had not gotten to him so quickly, he probably would not have lived."

For exhaustion, patients are kept in the bivouac hospital overnight to allow them a full night's rest with proper food and water. Most importantly, the forced rest is provided away from their compounds to avoid the distraction of worrying about their vehicles and race times. Sometimes medication is given to ensure the competitor gets some real sleep.

A death during the Dakar Rally is an especially difficult time for medical staff. The doctors and nurses come to know many of the competitors over the years, and losing one is very hard on the entire medical team. Dr. Pommerie related one case a few years ago, when, during registration, she met and interviewed a *moto* competitor from South Africa.

"His name was Elmer, which made me smile, as this was the name of a small elephant so familiar to me in the books I read to my children at home in France. Whenever I saw his name during the Rally, I would smile, until I learned he had died in an accident during that year's fourth special stage."

Dr. Pommerie's cartoon-elephant namesake was Elmer Symons, a thirty-year-old motorcycle mechanic and off-road racer. Born in Ladysmith, South Africa, in 1977, he was participating in his first Dakar as a privateer. He perished following a serious accident in Morocco only 142 kilometers into the fourth stage of the 2007 edition. In eighteenth place overall in the *moto* category, medical staff arrived by emergency helicopter only eight minutes after Elmer's Irritrack beacon was triggered, but unfortunately he had no vital signs when they arrived.

"I spoke with his family later," she told me. "I told them that I knew him, and that his death made me very, very sad."

If I were a Dakar competitor, I would want someone like Dr. Pommerie looking after me.

Elmer's story also revealed to me the closeness and camaraderie that endures within the extended Dakar community. During my three weeks with the Tamarugal team, I was posting some of my adventures on my website. After telling Elmer's story, I was contacted by his friend, Portuguese motorcyclist and adventurer Carlos Martins, who corrected me about a few facts and related more of Elmer's history and accomplishments. Mostly though he told me how wonderful a person Elmer was, and his fondness for Elmer's sense of adventure, his professionalism, and his lust for life.

"I miss Elmer very much, as do the wide circle of friends he had made within the motorcycling community," Carlos told me. "He was a terrific person." In Elmer's memory, Carlos and other friends embarked on a two-week bike trip from Lisbon, Portugal, retracing the 2007 Dakar route and into the day four stage, ending up in the Moroccan desert at the exact spot Elmer met his untimely death. At kilometer 142 of the desert track, they built a small stone cairn and painted an inscription honoring their friend, both looking west into the sunset, facing the direction Elmer would have been riding.

Carlos and his friends also learned firsthand about the dangers and the toughness of riding a Dakar. It took them three days, including stops for repairs, getting lost and stuck, and spending the night in the desert. They clocked just over twelve hours of actual riding time to complete the stage. Marc Coma, the winner of that stage in the 2007 Dakar, finished it in four hours and twenty-seven minutes. Quite a difference, and a real indication of just how fast Dakar riders are moving.

That evening I found myself at a makeshift picnic table, thinking about Elmer, the dangers of the Dakar, and wondering again what I was doing here. I was seated at one of about two hundred such tables extending out from the Dakar food service area under white canvas tents, rapidly becoming brown with all the swirling *polvo*. Beside me were six Russians, part of a team competing in the truck category. For some reason all the truck teams were big guys, swarthy and bald, well over six feet, paunchy, and anything but fit-looking. The language was guttural, dark, and fast, and they ate mountains of food, seemingly without chewing.

All around me were tables crowded with competitors, their team members, and the myriad of support people that made the Dakar run smoothly. Languages from over fifty countries were being spoken—Spanish, Portuguese, French, Japanese, Dutch, German, Finnish, Danish, Swedish, Turkish, Farsi, and Arabic—mostly by men.

There were a few female competitors on the Dakar—eleven at last count this year—with the rest coming from the medical and food services personnel, media, and the ever-present young lovelies working for Red Bull in their short shorts and halter tops. As the Red Bull girls might be all of sixteen years old, they could be flirted with, but their age was respected. They were lovely, and the Russians put down their forks to stare intently whenever one of them walked by.

As I sat at the table, listening to the Russians and admiring the Red Bull staff, I wondered what it must take to prepare and serve 2,200 breakfasts, 1,200 lunches, and 2,000 takeaway midday meals, as well as another almost 3,000 dinners every day for fourteen days. In planning these meals, the organizers must consider the nutritional needs of high-performance athletes hailing from many different cultural backgrounds, while at the same time dealing with almost all major global languages. They must also ensure sufficient supplies were on site, fresh and wholesome in fourteen different locations in three very different countries. They must do this today, and then again tomorrow some five hundred kilometers away in the middle of the desert, with no power, no water, and no sanitary systems.

For Fernando Mendilaharzu, Operations Manager for Sodexo Argentina and project manager for the food services on the Dakar Rally, it took almost eight months of discussions and planning to make sure everyone was fed at the right time, with the right menus, and with the right nutritional content to keep the Rally going. It was a monumental logistical and culinary task.

"We have three full crews operating during the Rally," he told me over a steak dinner we shared together one evening. "While one crew is cooking and serving meals tonight, a second full team is setting their kitchens up at the next bivouac, while the third begins the organization at the third in line. When the first crew is finished, it leapfrogs and moves on to the fourth. There are fifty-four people that travel and operate the three crews, along with another twenty managers, logistics people, technicians, drivers, and others. In addition, about twenty people are brought in at each bivouac primarily from local communities," he explained.

I asked him how the meals, which so far had been varied, interesting, and quite good, could be delivered and prepared in such a hostile environment.

"Food deliveries are arranged by truck each day, much brought from depots in Buenos Aries, Santiago, or Lima. However, we complement these deliveries with local purchases of bread, fruits, and vegetables to ensure freshness. One of the objectives of the Dakar organization is to support local economies, and we believe we meet this goal by hiring local folks to help out and by procuring local supplies."

I wondered about menu selections, as, with the French penchant for fine cuisine and sauces, there must be interesting negotiations when this sensibility and tradition came up against the local food culture of Argentina, Chile, and Peru. Despite what must be tough discussions, over the days I had been taking my meals in the Dakar bivouacs, I had been pleasantly surprised to see a mix of international foods—those Sodexo believed would be recognized and eaten by almost every culture around the world—combined with more regional cuisine, such as a beef *asado* in Argentina, *empanadas* and a seafood *chufe* in Chile, and regional seafood dishes such as *civiche* in Peru.

"For the French, God comes first, then your mother, and then food," Fernando explained to me. "It took lots of discussions and negotiations to bring our local cuisine into the mix, and we think the Dakar is much richer for this."

I think he is right.

CHAPTER NINE
GETTING TO KNOW FIVE COMPETITORS

With the extra rest day in Copiapó resulting from the cancelled stage due to the issues crossing the border, I had time to meet a few other Dakar Rally participants. During the stages and ensuing bivouacs, there was seldom any opportunity to sit down with competitors or their support crew. They were all working, studying, or resting, and I certainly did not want to disturb the routine all teams found necessary to complete their Dakar.

One young man who would be steeling himself for the final seven stages of this year's Dakar was twenty-five-year-old Daniel Gouët, the reason I was participating in this year's event. Daniel is a good-looking young man with long, wavy black hair, deep-blue eyes, and a friendly smile. My wife believes he is the perfect embodiment of a Latin movie matinee idol despite the fact, as she witnessed in the W Hotel in Santiago, that his shoulders, back, and arms are covered in tattoos, including the design of a motorcycle engine cylinder down one arm. Daniel was currently in fourteenth position overall in the *moto* category of the 2012 Dakar, and the top Chilean in the standings after the withdrawal of perennial favorite Chaleco Lopez yesterday due to a leg injury suffered in a fall. Seeing Chaleco's bike in the bivouac after the crash, it was a miracle he made it there.

Daniel began riding motorcycles at the age of ten, following in his father, Pedro's, footsteps, a lifelong enthusiast. The dream started when Daniel was eight and a family friend arrived at the Gouët home on his enduro bike. Daniel jumped on and looked around with his eyes shining. He was hooked.

He seemed a natural on enduro and motocross bikes, winning a number of national titles early in his career in various age and engine size groupings. Motocross is a competition on a fixed loop dirt track, usually about 1.5 kilometers long, with many jumps and steep curves. Enduro is similar to the Rally raid category, as it is outside in the country on challenging terrain, but it is much shorter than a Rally with a maximum of only three hundred kilometers. Both motocross and enduro use similar types of motorcycles. Rally raid, like the Dakar, is a completely different story.

As Daniel rose through the ranks of Chilean enduro and motocross competitions, a number of older peers, including Chaleco Lopez, now a good friend and mentor of Daniel's, suggested he would be a natural at Rally Raid, and in his first real test at the age of nineteen, he did very well. He saw clearly that his future was in the sport of Rally, and in 2010 he approached his parents to seek their permission to leave university after two years of study to turn professional, with the goal of participating in the Dakar in 2011.

To me, Daniel's father Pedro was clearly conflicted about his son's choice of career. As we spent time together following Daniel's progress through the 2012 Dakar, I could see how worried and apprehensive he was as we awaited Daniel's arrival at the numerous checkpoints and finish lines we were visiting. At each, Pedro peered anxiously into the swirling dust on the horizon, looking for signs that his son was safe. But he also had one eye on the stopwatch, wondering how he was doing, if he was moving up in the rankings, if he was performing to his expectations. For a parent, it must be a real dilemma.

"As a father, I wanted Daniel to finish school and perhaps settle into a safer career with more security," Pedro told me. "Yet this is the path he wants to take, and as a young man, we respect his decision and will support him any way we can." From watching Pedro follow his son's fortunes on this year's Dakar, he was certainly doing everything he could to let his son know his family was fully behind him.

Daniel's mother, Soledad, was equally conflicted. Soledad is a beautiful, petite woman, with curly blonde hair and blue eyes, a combination you rarely find in Chile. I have become good friends with her, Daniel's lovely sisters, and their extended family of aunts, uncles, cousins, and close friends, all following Daniel's progress with great interest.

"I worry a lot when Daniel is on a Rally," Soledad told me. "But it makes him so happy, and he is so determined to succeed in his chosen career, that we are all very proud to support him."

But what makes Daniel so good at the sport of Rally? Clearly physical strength and endurance are critical, as are a good sense of balance and an intuitive knowledge of how motorcycles behave in different situations. But Daniel possesses much more. He trains constantly, at least four days a week in the gym, working on his endurance and strength, with the rest of the week spent honing his skills in enduro, motocross, and Rally competitions across South America. He is also determined and mature beyond his twenty-five years, making decisions and taking actions that, to me, are the signs of a true future champion. He is calm in the face of adversity, takes everything in stride, and to watch him put on his headphones to zone everything else out while studying his Roadbook for the next day, you can't help but recognize how focused and committed he is.

As an example of this determination, during the August 2010 *Dos Sertoes* Rally in Brazil, the world's second longest Rally Raid after the Dakar, covering some five thousand kilometers in nine days, Daniel broke both his ankles in a horrendous crash during a particularly tricky section of the course. He was ultimately flown back to Santiago, where he underwent an operation to repair the injuries, and spent a month in bed recovering and then another month in rigorous physiotherapy. It was not until November 2010 that he could begin training in earnest for the January 2011 Dakar, his first, where he started in 148th position and finished 25th. Many would have given up well before.

But Daniel is much more than a competitor focused solely on the finish line. He also takes being a member of a team very seriously and goes out of his way to support, encourage, and help others. During this past year's Rally Chile, the country's top competition, he was running a clear first when one of his partners on the Tamarugal team, Claudio Rodrigo, riding in second place, had an accident close to the finish line. Instead of charging to the end, Daniel stopped, made sure Claudio was okay, and then borrowed a rope from a spectator and towed Claudio and his bike to the finish line. In another example, during the day seven stage of this year's Dakar, Daniel's mentor, Chaleco Lopez, suffered a crash that tore much of his *moto* apart and severely injured his leg, ultimately taking him out of the Rally. Again Daniel stopped, made sure Chaleco could ride, and then accompanied him for the final ten kilometers of the stage to ensure he got back safely. Daniel probably lost time and possibly a move further up in the overall standings by helping Chaleco, but he believed it was the right thing to do. Many others would have ridden past, happy with Chaleco's misfortune. But not Daniel Gouët.

Daniel also knows that he must depend on those around him if he is to truly succeed. When his father, Pedro, Rodrigo, and I booked rooms in a hotel in Chilecito, Pedro went to the bivouac to get Daniel, thinking he would benefit from a good night's sleep and a real shower. But Daniel declined, opting to stay with his team. If his team members had to sleep in tents and suffer cold showers, so would he. He would experience the same ups and downs as everyone around him.

No one is more important to Daniel's success than his mechanic, Marcello Verdugo, called "Chelo" by everyone. Chelo and Daniel have been together for over ten years now. As a mechanic for one of Chile's largest motorcycle dealers, and now an official mechanic with Honda Chile, Chelo goes wherever Daniel competes. Chelo is a big reason Daniel has done so well, and they have developed a very strong personal and professional relationship. When Daniel injured himself in Brazil in 2010, Chelo carried him piggyback through hospitals and airports to get him home to Santiago. Customs and border issues forced them to live in a small Brazil airport for three days, all the time Chelo looking after Daniel's health and well-being. They are partners in every sense of the word.

With Daniel's proven talents, his determination, and the continued support of family, friends, and teammates, he should go far, and there was a good chance Daniel Gouët could finish in the top ten of this year's Dakar Rally.

As I wandered through the Copiapó bivouac, it became apparent how huge an investment some of the companies and sponsors had made to compete in the Dakar. It's quite expensive simply to enter the Rally. A motorcyclist must pay thirteen thousand pounds as an entry fee, while the cars are charged twenty-two thousand pounds. But this is the least expensive aspect of participation. The two Rally cars entered by the Tamarugal team, for example, were worth approximately US$250,000 each, while adapting and preparing each of the four Honda motorcycles ran about US$80,000. Then add the cost of all the tools, parts, and supplies, as well as the support vehicles, including two huge Mercedes Benz transport trucks adapted for the Dakar, and then the seven Honda Ridgeline trucks we used to transport the crew. There were thirty-one people initially on our Tamarugal team, most being paid a salary and all their costs. It is a major and expensive endeavor.

It is a wonder that competitors enter the Dakar at all. Given the dangers and the significant costs involved in competing in the Rally, the prize money is almost insignificant. Total investments in the millions of dollars are made by the large teams, while the *loco* privateers invest their lifetime savings to compete. And for all that cost and effort, the winner in each category, in addition to bragging rights, only receives a smallish trophy and a cash prize of a paltry fifteen thousand pounds. Not a great return on investment.

And while the Tamarugal team was well staffed with all the necessary equipment and support, this investment and sponsorship paled in comparison to some of the really big teams. Many of these serious competitors aiming to win the Rally are supported by large teams of mechanics, trainers, massage therapists, sports psychologists, and other professionals dedicated to getting their pilots to the finish line as quickly and safely as possible. These teams are backed by huge sums of money provided by a host of sponsors wanting to be associated with a successful Dakar organization and have their names splashed in front of the more than ninety million people estimated to experience the Dakar on television, over the Internet, or live in South America.

A case in point is Team X-Raid, founded in 2002 to utilize the expertise of the BMW and the BMW Mini organizations to transform their production vehicles into high-performance Rally Raid cars. Initially using a BMW X5 vehicle, Team X-Raid quickly won a number of international Rally Raids. In 2006, they developed a newer, faster version using the BMW X3 and again finished strongly in numerous competitions, including the 2009, 2010, and 2011 editions of the Dakar in South America. In late 2010, Team X-Raid then launched the MINI All4 Racing group introducing a Rally Raid car based on the Mini Countryman you see everywhere. I had always thought the Mini was a bit of a toy, maybe something a hipster would use around town, and certainly not a performance vehicle capable of competing in the Dakar Rally. How wrong I was.

For the 2012 edition of the Dakar, Team X-Raid had entered five cars based on the Mini Countryman and three others based on the BMW X3, and the team had done extremely well so far. Stéphane Peterhansel, driving Mini car #302 for the team, is the most successful driver in the history of the Dakar, winning the Rally six times in the *moto* class before switching to cars in 1999. In the 2010 and 2011 editions of the Dakar in South America, he finished fourth, and so far through this year's Rally he had shared the lead through most of the stages.

Team X-Raid is a massive and daunting presence on the racecourse and in the Dakar bivouacs. It employs drivers and staff from all over the world, and it is one of the ultimate destinations for any competitive Rally Raid pilot or navigator at the peak of their careers. In the Team X-Raid compound you see people from Austria, Belgium, Brazil, Chile, France, Great Britain, Italy, Portugal, Poland, Spain, Sweden, and Germany. Each race vehicle has its own tractor and trailer assistance truck in the bivouac with a dedicated team of mechanics and other staff. Other big trucks in the T-4 class are allowed to support the team vehicles during the specials. They have their own medical staff, massage therapists, kitchen and catering, and, very cool to me, on top of each huge support truck and trailer are installed a line of small tents that pop up from the roofs where support staff can sleep above all the noise and out of the dust storms. All in all, Team X-Raid must have millions invested in the Dakar, and it shows.

On the complete opposite spectrum of the Dakar experience is another group of people, primarily in the *moto* category, who participate in the Rally all on their own. Called "privateers," they ride their bikes, fix them, and generally look after everything necessary to compete in a Dakar all by themselves. The privateers' goal is to finish the Dakar, and if they do well in the standings, maybe they can get a ride with a larger sponsored group like Team X-Raid in future years.

ZERO TO SIXTY

I spent the morning of the second rest day with three Turkish privateers, learning what it's like to participate solo in the Dakar and how it all works. All three pilots were clearly exhausted, and, despite two of their three *motos* now out of the competition due to engine failure, they were all glad they had made the effort.

Selcuk Bektas is a forty-six-year-old hobby rider and the main importer of KTM motorcycles in Turkey. This was his first Dakar, and he had been forced to abandon the Rally near the end of stage four. Kemal Merkit was riding in his eighth Dakar Rally. At fifty-one years old, he also worked with KTM in Turkey and is the most experienced in the Rally Raid world. Also from Turkey, Senkalayci Sakir was thirty years old and the country's top professional motorcycle racer, competing in enduro, motocross, superMX, and road events. This was also his first Dakar, and he was the only rider still in the competition.

Selcuk told me how the logistics worked for each privateer. There is an area in each bivouac called *Malles Motos* (the French word *Malles* roughly translates as "trunk"). All the privateers set up in the *Malles Motos* area close to a large truck sponsored by Total Energy that is organized to transport their boxes between the bivouacs. The privateers work on their bikes here, sleep here, and prepare for each day's stage from here. It is a bit crowded, you don't have much personal space, but everyone seems to get along and, in many instances, offer help to one another.

Selcuk told me that, in prior Dakars, the organizers had provided two trucks available for the privateers, but this year there was only one, forcing all the privateers to work even harder to keep going.

"The problem is the truck wants to leave early in the morning so that it can get to the next bivouac in time to set up before we arrive. That means they want to leave by 5:00 a.m., making it impossible for us to spend a few extra morning hours getting a bit of rest or more time on our bikes. Now if you have come in late at night from a long and difficult stage, and you then spend two or three hours changing tires and oil, fixing other things on your *moto*, you don't get much sleep, as you have to get up around 4:00 a.m. to prepare your box for shipment. You are then very tired for that day's stage, it affects your performance, and you arrive to the *Malles Moto* even later that next day or night. It becomes a cumulative and vicious circle of less and less sleep and poorer and poorer performance, only to make sure your box gets transported."

It was also interesting to understand what happens when a *moto* breaks down in the middle of a stage. Selcuk crashed his KTM during stage four between San Juan and Chilecito in Argentina. As a result of the crash, his radiator lines were cut and, unknown to him, leaked coolant fluid until his engine seized about ten kilometers from the finish. As it was getting dark, he declined an offer from a couple of other riders for a tow to the finish. He pressed the blue intercom button on his emergency Irritrack system, which dispatched a medical team to him. They arrived, ensured he had sufficient water, and provided him with a couple of boxed lunches for food.

The Dakar has a number of "sweeper trucks," large trucks that move out onto the racecourse well after the competitors are all supposed to be safely in the next bivouac, ensuring no individual or incapacitated vehicle has been left behind. But on some stages, as happened on this one, there were quite a few riders and *motos* damaged earlier in the stage.

"They told me the sweeper truck might be by in three hours, maybe the next morning, or even possibly the following day," Selcuk told me. "'You mean I may have to wait here for two days?' I asked them." The answer was yes.

Selcuk then pointed out to the medical crew that it was starting to rain and, with a possible storm on the horizon, it could be dangerous for him to be abandoned outdoors and alone for possibly two days. After consulting with Paris and race headquarters, the medical team was instructed to transport Selcuk out of the desert and to the bivouac in Chilecito. But it took two days to get his bike out of the sand.

His partner, Kemal, had better luck. Sand got into his motor, perhaps due to a faulty air filter, seizing his engine in a particularly difficult area of deep desert on day six. Because they were not sure the sweeper truck could get to him without also becoming bogged down in the sand, the organizers arranged to have Kemal and his *moto* evacuated by helicopter. The retired bikes were then transported to Lima, Peru, by the ASO to be put on the ship carrying all the European vehicles back to Le Havre, France, after the Rally, where Selcuk and Kemal would have to make arrangements to get them back to Turkey.

Selcuk estimated that, all in, including his KTM motorcycle, the total cost for each to participate in the Dakar was about forty thousand pounds. The magnitude of the cost really depends on the quality of the bike used, he told me.

"Because of very high import duties in Turkey, we had to use production KTM enduro bikes and modify them as best we could for the demands of the Dakar. The proper KTM bike for the Dakar would have cost almost €40,000 alone, before any of our other expenses, and there was no way we could afford that expense. We did receive some in-kind sponsorship from a number of parts and clothing suppliers, and the Turkish Motorcycle federation paid each of our €13,000 entrance fees to encourage more participation in biking and Rallying in Turkey. Still, it was a lot money to only complete three stages of the Dakar and almost get stuck alone in the desert for three days with only water and a bag lunch." He smiled.

But talking to these guys, you really got a sense of the passion the Dakar brings out in people. The proof is the fact that they all wanted to come back next year and hopefully, with the experience gained though the 2012 Dakar, do much better.

Utilizing another strategy to compete in his first Dakar was David Bensadoun, the only Canadian in this year's Rally. David was forty-one years old, the son of the founder and a Vice President of Aldo Shoes, an international company that has grown to include more than 1,600 stores in sixty-five countries. Born and raised in Montreal to a Moroccan French Jewish father and a Scottish Protestant mother, he has been in love with motor sports since his dad taught him to ride a Yamaha 100 Enduro motorcycle at the age of ten. After completing college at Cambridge in England, he and a friend rode their bikes through Europe and then south through Africa for two months all the way to Cape Town. Returning to Canada, he started off-road *moto* racing, working hard at the sport for the next twelve years.

"I was a strong B rider and always finished races, but I am a really big guy, and it was tough to excel at the sport," he told me. He competed in the New England Enduro Championships, the Quebec Championships, and ultimately the Canadian National Championships for Enduros.

Before marrying and settling down to a career with his family company, he toured South America by motorcycle, starting in Caracas, Venezuela, and traveling to Tierra del Fuego before finishing in Buenos Aires. Perhaps a precursor of a Dakar to come?

As a child and a young man, he spent many Christmas and New Year's holidays in France with his extended family, and he became familiar with the Dakar as it traveled through Paris past his uncle's home on its customary route south through the city. He remembers when he was ten or twelve, being on the balcony of his uncle's apartment and watching all the Dakar trucks, cars, and motorcycles pass in front of the crowds below. The Rally was also well covered by all the local magazines, newspapers, and carried live on television. He became hooked, and, as his motorcycle racing career and his bike travels increased his skills, he dreamed to experience a Dakar himself in the *moto* category.

But as he became a little older and a little wiser, and married with three children under the age of five, the dangers of riding a motorcycle on the Dakar weighed heavily. With his family's blessing and support, in 2005 he began to train for participation in the Dakar auto category. Over the next few years he gained valuable experience and was all set to enter the 2008 edition of the Dakar, when it was canceled due to the terrorist threats. He was waiting for the Rally to return to Africa, but after understanding the similarity of challenges present in the South American editions, he put his name forward to enter the 2012 Dakar.

A number of competitors use the exposure and global following of the Dakar to raise money for charities of their choice, and David is a case in point. As a key component of his dream to complete the Dakar, David raised more than $250,000 for AIDS research.

David's car was called a Desert Warrior and was built by the English firm Rally Raid UK, a company that specializes in helping individual Dakar competitors economically participate in the Rally. The company will construct a vehicle to your own specifications, handle all the logistics and registration work, and provide all the mechanics and other support necessary to start and, hopefully, finish a Dakar. Rally Raid had three vehicles in the 2012 edition. One car had to drop out a month before the Dakar even started, with the second retiring on day two. David's car cost him €105,000, with the Rally Raid support package another €75,000. It's not inexpensive to compete in the Dakar.

When I first met David during the registration process, I was struck by how big a guy he really is. At six feet five inches tall and weighing in at over three hundred pounds, he towered over the rest of the field. The folks who built his car laughingly told me they had to extend his cab by six inches, widen it by five inches, and add extra headroom just to get him into the vehicle.

During the rest day, I met with him to find out what it was like to participate in his first Dakar. He had started the Rally in Mar del Plata in 157th position, and when I caught up with him, significant vehicle attrition and his preparations and experience had moved him up into 39th place. He described for me what had occurred the previous day, one that was quite typical for a Dakar stage, he claimed.

"The first thing to happen was a guy forcing me into the ditch after I signaled I wanted to pass with my Sentinel device. He clearly did this on purpose, but what could I do? We now had two flat tires and a ruined wheel rim, but we had to keep going. Then, eight kilometers later, we approached another car, and, because of all the clouds of dust, I could not see properly trying to pass, and we got high centered on a huge boulder with two of our wheels off the ground. We had to use our hydraulic rams to get the car back on all four wheels, but in doing so we bent the shaft of the ram. We then took the ram apart to fix it, as we were not sure if we would need it again, but because we are not allowed to leave garbage on the course, we approached some locals in pickup trucks and asked them to dispose of the waste hydraulic fluid and wrecked parts. All of this took a lot of time.

"And then a little later we got stuck twice in the sand dunes, became a bit lost, and arrived into the bivouac well after dark. But it was not as bad as it could have been. I have a great navigator—Patrick Beaulé has competed in a number of Rally Raids on motorcycles, and navigating on a bike teaches you a lot. Without Patrick's experience and sense of calm, it could have been a lot worse. A typical Dakar day," he sighed.

I asked him why he did this—put his career and family on hold to risk his life for something as intangible as participating in a Dakar Rally.

"I love the whole aspect of Rally Raid that is about self-reliance, your machine, the preparation, the endurance, making it through tough sections of a course, the problem solving, all of it. Each day on the course, we make tons of mistakes, all of which should be in our control to avoid. If we can correct just some of those, I am sure we could move up another ten places in the rankings. Take today, for example, when the driver we were trying to pass pushed us into the rocks, trashing two of our tires. We should have waited to pass in a section where there was more room. But we were in race mode, we got a little mental, and we made a mistake. If one more flat tire had occurred, we might have had to retire from the Rally. That's when the Dakar can really bite you, when you drive too fast and you stop thinking clearly.

"But mostly I love the Dakar and rallying because it takes me out of my regular life. I sometimes find regular life so boring, and I have always done different things to get away from that life. I knew I was headed towards a Dakar, but I didn't want to be simply that guy who could afford to write the check but did not really have the right to be there. For the last four years I have been actively planning and preparing for this Dakar. I did two rallies in Morocco to learn how to drive in the dunes, I took a lot of time to learn the mechanics of my car, I carefully went through as many scenarios as I could and interviewed many other Dakar drivers about their experiences, all aimed at helping me understand what tools and supplies I might need to deal with any and all possibilities. So far, it has worked. If someone told me before I started that I would be in thirty-ninth position today, I would have told them they were crazy. But here we are, and it's all down to our preparation, my co-driver and navigator, Patrick, the support I receive from the folks at Rally Raid UK, and thinking things through—most of the time. Next year I hope we will do even better."

Yes, he told me, he planned to return for the 2013 edition of the Dakar.

All during this unscheduled second rest day, I had been feeling a profound sense of homesickness. I missed my wife, my family, my friends, and the comforts of home. I was more tired than I had ever been, and after two weeks of noisy sleepless nights in a hot sleeping bag within a small, claustrophobic tent, long days of driving, and the ceaseless excitement experienced following the Dakar and its competitors, two days of rest forced the adrenaline pump to slow down. I was dirty, so very dirty from the *polvo* that gets into everything you own and the sweat that builds up following days and days of extremely hot temperatures. My brain hurt from dealing with everything in a language I did not fully understand. The thought of another week was almost too much to bear.

After years of motorcycle traveling, I recognize this letdown, and it happens frequently. You are moving, driven by the adventure, the new sights and senses, but when you stop for a rest, you wonder why you are doing this to yourself, taking yourself away from family and friends and comforts. When you stop, you don't want to go on. You just want to go home.

And after two weeks with the team and the Dakar community, I could certainly leave now—I had accomplished a lot, learned a lot, seen a lot—and I was sure no one would really miss me. But the job, my job, would not be done, and I was sure I would be letting Rodrigo down, who was depending on me as a co-driver for the truck. Also, as I had been told countless times, the real Dakar only began in Copiapó, as competitors faced the challenges and dangers of the sand dunes in northern Chile and southern Peru. The next week would separate the men from the boys, and I wanted to be there. I packed my sleeping bag and gear, threw it in the back of the truck, sought help yet again to fold my accursed tent, and headed out for the final drive to Lima.

CHAPTER TEN
THE DESERT DUNES: THE REAL DAKAR BEGINS

Picture yourself here. You are sitting astride your powerful, custom-designed, off-road motorcycle, helmet and goggles tilted back on your head, wiping the perspiration from your face with a bandana. You are on the very peak of a massive mountain of sand maybe a thousand meters high, the knobby front wheel of your bike facing down the steep slope in front of you, the rear wheel on the back side, sitting in the rut you made ascending the sand mountain. You are looking around, wondering what you should do now, where you should go next.

All around you, in every direction and to every horizon you can see, are vast tracts of desert—more mountains and dunes of sand, carved by the wind into the valleys you need to find to get back on track. It is quite beautiful, really, but you know from experience that the sand can be very deceptive and very dangerous. What might appear to be a solid slope of firm sand could actually be so loose any vehicle would immediately become completely bogged down, wheels spinning uselessly and digging even deeper into the surface if powered to try and move you forward. There might be a field of that evil *feche feche* at the bottom, deep piles of talcum powder like sand that provides absolutely no traction whatsoever. It's like swimming in soft, deep, fine dust, but smellier. You have fallen over in that stuff many times already today, and been forced to push your bike out to find more solid ground.

But when it works, when everything comes together, when your muscle memory is able to respond to the months of training and practice you have undergone, when, to use a corny and oft-misused phrase, you are truly one with your motorcycle and the sand, it is sublime, like skiing or boarding in the powder snow of your winter youth. You ride up the dunes effortlessly, finding the right track to the top, and then surf down the steep other side, moving steadily and quickly over the course.

But when it goes wrong, it is a nightmare of effort, the bike slewing out from under you, causing you to tumble and roll, unable to stop, back down the dune you have been trying to climb, or sliding your bike and body into rocks or those mounds of small, dense bush-like vegetation with the long, sharp, and thick needle-like thorns that can tear through whatever protective equipment you are wearing to scar your flesh.

It is also hot, so very, very hot, and getting hotter—well over 40°C—with the sun beginning its descent into the west, adding to your worries that it is starting to get late. Water conservation is critical now, as this region has not seen rain, or any precipitation really, in many, many decades. And any rain that might fall will only evaporate before reaching the hot and arid ground. It is well recognized as the driest place on earth, and you are lost smack-dab in the middle of it.

From your vantage point, high on top of the ridge, you cannot see any other vehicles, which is really not good news. The trick when you are lost is to find someone else's tracks and follow them, hoping that they too have not mislaid their way. Because if you run out of fuel or, God forbid, injure yourself in a fall from exhaustion or dehydration, or both, it could be a day or two before anyone can come to your rescue, if they can find you at all. You have invested far too much time, effort, and hard-earned cash to be beaten now, so close to the finish.

Suddenly, you spy a speck moving through the valley far below you, throwing up a long trail of dust behind it. It's another motorcycle, hopefully on track and moving in the right direction. You immediately pull on your helmet and goggles, kick your bike into gear, and slalom down the steep sand slope to follow him—because the real Dakar had just begun today, in the deserts of northern Chile.

Stage seven of the 2012 Dakar would see all of the competitors facing these challenges. Following the two rest days in the Copiapó bivouac, the Rally moved north toward Antofagasta with the longest day and the longest stage of this year's event, including liaison sections of 245 kilometers and a special of 477 kilometers. The special ran primarily along stone and sand track, and it promised to be a fast day, though large boulders strewn along the trails could prove problematic. Later in the day, the 2012 Dakar would visit its first real test in sand.

We waited at checkpoint three for the *motos*, and soon Marc Coma, the overall leader, pulled in, had his card stamped, refueled his bike, and took his mandatory fifteen-minute break. These pauses are designed to ensure riders get some water and a bit of a breather, and don't push themselves too hard on these long stages. Coma started the stage two minutes before his next competitor, but it was a good nine minutes before the next rider crossed through the checkpoint. Apparently a few riders once again got lost and bogged down in a muddy river. All four Tamarugal riders came through just fine, with Daniel Gouët maintaining his unofficial overall fourteenth position.

Rodrigo and I took the truck to watch riders come down one very fast section after the checkpoint, and to wait for the leading cars to take the same path. As we were waiting, a big, heavy BMW 1200RS motorcycle fully loaded with luggage came flying over a hill right on the racecourse. I imagine the rider thought a better viewpoint could be found farther down the track and if they hurried, they would be out of the way before another rider came along. How they could think they would not encounter a race vehicle is beyond anyone's guess. As the big heavy bike crested the hill and started down, its front wheel suddenly started to slew in the deep *polvo,* and, in seconds, the rider was flying over the front with the bike crashing across the track, throwing parts everywhere. The rider was just off the course and not moving.

I jumped out of the truck as I saw the accident happen and ran over. I checked the rider, a woman in her late fifties, and although she was complaining of a sore shoulder and arm, I could see she was alive, moving, and conscious. My next concern was the big bike blocking the course below the hill and out of sight of approaching competitors. If one of the *moto* riders hit the crashed bike at the speeds they travel, it would be a serious accident. I tried to lift it up but kept slipping in the *polvo*. I noticed one of the injured riders' friends sitting on his bike, watching me. What was he thinking? I wondered. I shouted for him to help me, and leisurely he parked his bike on its side stand and strolled over to help. I could have killed him. We managed to get the bike upright. I got it started and feathered the clutch to get it off the course. I told the friend to immediately move it farther away from the racetrack.

By now the woman's other friends were coming back to help, apparently a group of older US citizens on rented BMW bikes following the Dakar for a few days. They were standing around talking to her as she continued to lie on the ground just beside the race route, wondering what to do. I told them that she had to be moved right away, as, with the more powerful, much wider and faster cars coming, anything could happen. If she was that close to the track, and any race vehicle veered a bit left over the hill, they could all be killed.

"Can't you go to the race officials and ask them to slow down past here?" one of the woman's friends whined.

Right. As if that would happen. They moved her farther away, and we left.

Now I really hoped the woman was okay, but she should not have been riding such a big bike, she should not have been riding off-road in the sand and *polvo*, she should definitely not have been on the actual racecourse, and she should not have been going so fast—dumb decisions that could have caused serious injuries to a lot more people. What was she thinking? I don't think she was thinking.

Spectators need to be very aware of how dangerous the Dakar can be in full race mode. Every year fans are killed or badly injured trying to get too close to the course or take that perfect picture of a car in the air, only to have it land on them. Rodrigo was closely missed by Robby Gordon's Hummer two days ago. You never know where these vehicles are going to come from, and you have no idea how fast they are traveling. If you come to experience the Dakar, please, please be careful.

Spectators particularly have to be cautious when the truck competitors move through any viewing zone on the special course. While you may be lucky to dodge a more maneuverable *moto* or car in race mode, getting out of the way of one of these huge and heavy Rally race truck behemoths is a completely different matter.

While I fully understand the inclusion of the *moto*, quad, and car categories in the Dakar Rally, I was really having trouble wrapping my mind around the truck classification. You have probably seen these massive vehicles traveling at high speed being launched into the air over a sand dune. Inside are three pilots—a driver, a navigator, and a mechanic. At a minimum three people are needed in the event anything breaks down on these trucks, especially a flat tire. The tire alone is about five feet high. In the back of the trucks are spare tires, a couple of sand ramps for when they get stuck, shovels, and some other small tools. Weight is the enemy in the truck class, and everything is done to shave kilos, including cutting off the ends of screws, if possible. Since the 2010 Dakar, the trucks have been limited to 150 kilometers per hour on the specials. It's scary.

The cabs of these big racing trucks are very sophisticated and very complex. The three people sit about twelve feet up in the air—you need a six-step ladder to get into the cab. The driver does not have many distractions, other than a small video screen to see what is behind him, and a second set of cameras to watch down the sides of the truck should a mirror be ripped off, a common occurrence. The mechanic sits in the middle, monitoring essential items such as engine and oil temperature, tire pressure, as well two video monitors watching each of the front and rear axles and differentials under the truck. He can also request up to sixteen different tire pressure combinations to adjust for different types of terrain—soft for sand, hard for pavement, and everything in between. The navigator sits in the third seat by the passenger window with two redundant Tripy systems; two, three, or four odometers; the Irritrack GPS device; and other navigation aids; in addition to the Dakar required safety systems. When the trucks are designed, all unessential gauges and devices are removed from the cabs, but it sure looked complicated to me. It also seemed like a tight fit. I hoped the three guys liked each other and wore deodorant.

The Dakar truck category was originally invented so the large factory teams could have some form of support for their cars on the race specials. The rule in the Dakar is that a vehicle on a special cannot receive assistance from anyone or anything except others who are also racing on the same special. Thus, these large trucks were entered, full of parts and supplies, to help their brothers and sisters competing in *motos* and cars on the course. But, being guys with big engines under them, they too started to race, and the trucks were then included as an official Dakar category with its own prizes and awards.

One of the dynasties in the sport of truck racing is the large and extended de Rooy family from Holland. The godfather of the truck class is Jan de Rooy, the owner of a large transportation company in Europe. Through his affiliation with DAF Trucks, the largest manufacturer in Holland, he entered his first Dakar Rally in 1982. It was a minor disaster, but he made it to the finish. He then began to engineer and build his own trucks in collaboration with DAF, and he was the first to design and build a chassis with two separate engines to drive each of the front and rear axles and two cabs to house the driver, mechanic, and navigator. With this innovative system, he won the Dakar in 1987 and became a hero in Holland. His nickname was "Luc"—the bear. He is a large and imposing man, like the Russians I ate with a few days before.

The next year he engineered a new truck that was so fast it was actually overtaking some of the leading cars on the Rally, traveling more than two hundred kilometers per hour. And the trucks back then were much larger than the trucks entered into today's Dakar! However, Jan's second truck suffered a major accident during one Dakar, and his copilot was killed. As a result of potential bad publicity arising from the fatality, DAF decided to leave the Dakar, as did Jan. Also as a result of this accident, in 1989 there was no truck category, and in 1990 the category reappeared with more stringent rules and regulations aimed primarily at safety.

Jan's son, Gerard, then became interested in driving trucks in the Dakar. When he was eighteen, he convinced his dad to build another truck and enter the 2001 edition. The new truck was built to old designs, and while it did reasonably well, it was not very competitive. The father-and-son team entered again in 2002, with Gerard competing on his own in 2003. In that race, on the stage after the rest day, they crashed and the entire cab was ripped off the truck. Fortunately no one was hurt, and they competed in the next three Dakars.

For the 2012 Rally, the de Rooy family entered five trucks, all built and designed with the Italian firm Iveco, led by thirty-year-old Gerard. The team was largely the same as his father built in the 1980s, with Gerard's dad serving as team manager. One of the trucks was also being driven by Hans Stacey, Gerard's cousin. Hans won the truck category Dakar in 2007. Supporting the five trucks in the Rally, two of which were in the T4 category as assistance, was a team of thirty-eight people, another four transport trucks with parts and supplies, and a couple of jeeps. Each truck in the competition cost between four hundred thousand and five hundred thousand pounds to design, build, and support. In total, the team believed they had invested over five million pounds to compete in this year's Dakar.

Gerard was lucky to be here. He had broken his back twice in Rally-related accidents, and he had designed a new style of truck for this year's competition with a torpedo nose instead of the traditional flat front which provided much superior visibility directly in front of the vehicle. For Gerard, his radical design placed the engine behind the cab, causing less bounce and more comfort for someone with back injuries.

Watching these trucks compete in the sand dunes was astonishing. They moved so quickly, yet they looked like giant animals rearing over the mountains of sand. Because they can be top-heavy, they often tip over, and it takes another truck competitor or T-4 vehicle to right them. They also create deep, deep tracks and massive clouds of *polvo* as they race through the course. Most cars and *motos* do their very best to stay ahead of them. Seeing one of these beasts approach in your rearview mirror can invoke significant terror.

CHAPTER ELEVEN
WINNING AT ANY COST

The Antofagasta bivouac at the end of day seven was quite pretty. Nestled on a beach just north of the city, we looked out on the Pacific Ocean with the sun setting behind bright-red clouds shining onto a large rocky point jutting out into the bay. Fresh ocean breezes replaced the *polvo* of the last few days, and it was relatively cool compared to the high temperatures we had been enduring in northern Argentina and Copiapó. If it was not for the Russian team close to my tent working all night on their big trucks with generators howling, hammers banging, and machinery running, as well as the deep, guttural voices discussing their repairs, I might have had a good sleep.

Life in the bivouac was now becoming more comfortable and interesting. I felt as though I was fitting in, a part of the team and of the extended Dakar family. I was recognizing many of the faces and teams now, and many exchanged friendly waves with me as I continually got lost, very lost. Take today, for example.

When we arrived in the bivouac around 4:00 p.m., many of the compounds had not been set up. In fact, our large transport truck had not yet arrived. We staked out an area with our two Honda Ridgeline pickups, and I went to the media center to do some work. When I emerged a few hours later, all the other teams had arrived with their race and support vehicles, and the landscape was completely different. I had no idea where our vehicles were located. The same thing happened when I finally found our area and then had to return to the bathrooms or the dining area—I couldn't remember where they were located. Thus, I employed the "wandering around" strategy. The benefit of this plan was that I ultimately did find my destination, but I also got to see more teams and perhaps strike up a conversation, hear a few stories, and learn more about the Dakar.

On one walk back to our compound today, I spent a few minutes at Chaleco Lopez's compound to hear what had happened with his accident and to see his bike. It was a mess. The entire front end of the Aprilia was bent backward and to the side. All of the gauges and navigation equipment were gone, with the various wires and brackets hanging forlornly into the ruined cowling. The coolant radiators were missing, and the right side of the bike was severely dented, with most of the paint and decals illegible. No wonder he damaged his right leg in the crash, as he must have torn all this gear off the bike as he flew over the handlebars. He was very fortunate to have survived this high-speed accident with only an injured leg.

While talking to Chaleco's mechanics, Alain Duclos came over and told me about his adventures on the Copiapó-to-Antofagasta stage. Alain rode on the same Aprilia team with Chaleco. Duclos's bike had broken down in the sand that day, they believed because of an electrical problem, and, after taking the seat, rear spare gas tanks, and a few other parts off the bike unsuccessfully to find the problem, he had left to go in search of some help.

"When I returned," Duclos related with a wry grin, "the seat and spare gas tanks had been stolen. Believe me, it is impossible to ride a Dakar route without a seat and sufficient fuel to finish the stage. Hoping against hope I might find my missing parts, I wandered around the area until I came upon some local race fans on motorcycles. Somehow I managed to talk to them in my broken Spanish, and unbelievably one loaned me the seat off his older Honda, which I was able to strap on to my Aprilia with cable ties and duct tape. Another of the guys gave me a full plastic gas container and a backpack to hold it. With this spare fuel strapped to my back, and an ill-fitting seat that constantly threatened to spill me onto the ground, I was able to finish the stage, arriving in the bivouac around 2:00 a.m. My team only had three hours to make the repairs, but they pulled it off and I was ready to start out again at 5:30 that morning.

"I hope I can find the guys that helped me out—without them I would still be in the desert waiting for the sweeper truck!"

Andrés Carevic is another interesting story. A captain in the Chilean Army, he was given official leave from the military and an investment from the Chilean government to compete in the *moto* category with a small team supporting his Yamaha motorcycle. Named "Captain Rally" in Chile, and a big crowd favorite, he was in his first Dakar and, while full of spirit and working hard, was near the back of the pack. On the Copiapó loop stage on day seven, he too had engine troubles late in the day. While he was trying to fix his bike, Etienne Lavigne, the Dakar organization director, saw him from his helicopter. Carevic was a sentimental favorite of Lavigne's, because both men came from a military background. Captain Rally's participation in the Dakar was designed to bring some much needed positive publicity for the Chilean armed forces, especially after the disrepute they garnered during the dictatorship of Augusto Pinochet.

Lavigne landed his helicopter close to where Carevic was broken down and suggested Captain Rally really should retire from the competition. It was getting late at night, he was well down in the standings, and no one was sure he could get his bike started again. Carevic refused to quit, they argued for a bit, and Lavigne left.

But Lavigne remained worried and a few hours later, with some water and food, returned to find Carevic in the same predicament. But again Carevic refused to quit, and Lavigne departed in frustration. Carevic then settled down for a few hours' rest and finally managed to push his bike to the bivouac and start the next day. He was still in 118th position of the 120 *motos* remaining in the competition, but what a guy.

There are also a few stories that, perhaps, do not show some of the competitors in the best light. During the Copiapó-to-Antofagasta stage, a number of elite *moto* riders became seriously stuck in the mud of a dried-out riverbed. Among them were the French rider and past Dakar champion Cyril Despres, in second place overall at the time, and the Portuguese rider Helder Rodrigues, holding down third place just behind Despres.

The mud looked like concrete on the video highlights, sticking to everything and making movement almost impossible. You could see how frustrated the riders were getting; they struggled to pull their bikes out of the quagmire, enduring the heat and the *polvo*, believing their

Dakar dreams were slipping away. I was told Rodrigues, in the spirit of cooperation, walked down the riverbed and helped Despres yank his bike out of the mud. But as he returned to his bike, fully expecting to receive the same favor, it was rumored that Despres just sped away. Like the car that forced David Bensadoun into the ditch a few days before, for some of the elite competitors, winning was everything.

The day eight special was again a long one for the Dakar competitors. It ran 556 kilometers, almost the entire distance between the start and finish bivouacs; however, in the middle there was a long neutralization route where the competitors had to drive slowly in respect for the environmentally sensitive salt flats aptly named *El Salar de Miraje*. The Dakar organization is very cognizant of the environmental impact the Rally can have, and works closely with local governments to ensure any environmentally sensitive areas and heritage sites are avoided. In addition, the Rally offsets its carbon emissions through an annual US$200,000 donation to the *Madre de Dios* environmental project, an organization that is preserving forest within the Amazon Basin in Peru. To date, the project has saved almost 120,000 hectares of forest that otherwise would have been destroyed.

In addition to their environmental contributions, the Dakar has provided decades of support to countries in Africa through which it used to pass. Over the last four years that the Rally has run in South America, the organization has contributed over half a million dollars to *Un Techo para mi Pais* (A Roof for my Country), building more than 250 emergency houses in Argentina, Chile, and Peru, helping to integrate families into their new communities through literacy development programs and donated computer equipment.

Competitors are also encouraged to take part with vehicles that use renewable energy, and for the first time the 2012 Dakar saw a car powered by electricity compete in the Rally.

The day eight stage ended coming down an exceptionally steep and long mountain of sand into the Iquique bivouac. And when I say it was a mountain of sand, it was *big*. The riders, cars and trucks, and following helicopters looked like tiny ants trailing lines of dust as they fell down the hill into the bivouac. I don't know how they did it, but they all seemed to arrive safely. Daniel Gouët had a good day, finishing twenty-second but moving up in the overall standings one place to thirteenth.

As I watched the *moto* riders navigate down the steep sand dunes coming into Copiapó, I was very cognizant of how different it was to ride an off-road motorcycle than a conventional street or touring bike. I had been riding motorcycles for more than thirty years. but I had never ridden a proper off-road bike, or known how to correctly address the challenges of navigating in deep sand and gravel, across rutted tracks or steep and narrow twisting dirt trails, or what to do when encountering fallen logs or large rocks at high speed.

As I learned, off-road *motos*, the type used on the Dakar, are much lighter and have a shorter wheel span than the road bikes I was accustomed to riding. You adopt a much different posture, sitting very far forward on the seat, directly over the foot pegs, with your elbows elevated and extended. It is like sitting on a child's swing with your arms holding onto the supporting chains. It is not very comfortable, and it is very alien to an experienced road rider like me. However, it places much more of the rider's weight over the front wheel, an important aspect for control and braking. And unlike road riding, where the front brake is the primary tool for stopping, off-road bikes use the rear brake much more frequently. It is also critical to ride on your toes, positioning the front of the foot on the foot pegs rather than on the instep, as on a road bike. This posture keeps you much closer to the rear brake and gear-shifting levers. If you ride the "road bike" way, there is a real chance the front of your foot will angle down and be in peril of amputation by a tree, stump, or rock. Yikes!

Braking skills and the bike's behavior under braking are also quite different. Because you are positioned so far forward, there is much less of your weight on the rear of the motorcycle, which allows it to slip from side to slide in the various loose surfaces encountered during a Dakar. When braking, the rear of the bike will skid and slew around, and it is crucial to keep your eyes up and looking forward, ensuring you steer the bike in the direction you want to go.

Another major difference from road riding—and you see this constantly during the Dakar—is the necessity to stand up on the foot pegs of the motorcycle with your legs slightly bent. You hold onto the bike with your thighs and calves, squeezing the top of the bike with your legs to permit your upper body to be loose and flexible. This position permits only the motorcycle's suspension system to absorb the bumps and rattles, and not your body. When you can't see a bump or gully, you have to instinctively feel the ride and trust the bike to handle the rough terrain.

Cornering an off-road bike at speed can also be challenging, especially in loose surfaces like sand and gravel. If you utilize conventional techniques, like turning the front wheel or leaning into the turn, the bike will almost always slide out from under you. The trick here is to enter the turn at speed, fully engage the clutch, and then slam on the rear brake to force the rear of the motorcycle to slide out and point you the right way. The clutch is then engaged, the brake released, and you accelerate forward.

As I watched the techniques and skills used by the *moto* competitors, I had a newfound respect for what they were doing. Riding a bike off-road is exhausting even for short periods of time, and to perform day after day in the high temperatures and blazing sun of South America is nothing short of heroic.

CHAPTER TWELVE
"FECHE FECHE": THE BANE OF A BIKER'S EXISTENCE

Stage nine, the special on the route from Iquique north to Arica near the border between Chile and Peru, provided some excitement and some drama today. The 377-kilometer special first looped south away from Iquique back toward the route taken yesterday, although today it would follow along the Pacific coast, with spectacular views of the ocean, driving through more than one hundred square kilometers of open and untracked sand dunes.

The special then turned north, and competitors would face their first extended encounter with what rallyists call *feche feche*. This is the bane of a motorcyclist's existence—fine, fine sand, almost like talcum powder in consistency and texture, and when it lays in deep piles it is almost impossible to drive through. Your front wheel becomes bogged down, slews everywhere, and, unless you are experienced navigating the stuff, falls are frequent. In my motorcycle travels through South America, I have encountered small amounts of *feche feche* on back country dirt roads, and almost every time I have slowed down too much and my bike has fallen away under me, fortunately with no lasting ill effects. But the Dakar *moto* competitors would be hitting vast piles of this dangerous surface toward the end of the special, and there would be a number of costly spills. If they managed to make it through, riders then faced a 317-kilometer liaison to the Arica bivouac.

For the Tamarugal *moto* team, the great news on day nine was the performance of Claudio "Burro" Rodriguez, who turned in a very fast time, finishing sixteenth on the stage, his best ride so far on this Dakar. I was watching at a spectator zone late in the special, providing an excellent view of the riders as they traversed down the side of a steep cliff into a rock- and sand-filled gully. Two riders had preceded Burro down the ridge when he suddenly veered off the track and ran full speed down the near-vertical sandy cliff, bisecting the safer route and pulling onto the straight track well ahead of the other two bikes. It was a daring and dangerous move, but it worked. The only other competitor to try the same strategy was Robby Gordon in his big orange Hummer, who employed the same tactic to pull ahead of his Mini competition.

Which brings me to the drama today. The Dakar judges, after appeal, decided to disqualify Gordon from the 2012 Dakar Rally due to a nonapproved engine ventilation system. Appalled at the decision, Gordon and his team were vigorously protesting and were determined to continue racing until the outcome of their formal appeal was determined.

Robby Gordon attracts a lot of attention on the Dakar. Celebrating his forty-third birthday on the second day of the 2012 Rally, his on-the-edge driving; his bigger-than-life, bright-orange Hummer car; his brash, in-your-face personality; and his legendary and often controversial record as a driver of numerous types of road sports all combined to make him a top favorite with the crowds.

Gordon is best known for his participation in US NASCAR racing, where he has three wins and thirty-nine top-ten finishes in the Sprint Cup Series since his debut in 1991. He has competed in 54 Nationwide Series races, 107 times in his Champ Car career, and run 8 times in the CART open-wheel IndyCar Series. In addition to his car racing, he also has four career Craftsman Truck Series races under his belt, and has recently formed a partnership with BIGFOOT 4x4 to build and participate in monster truck events, primarily to sell merchandise under his Speed Energy brand. An entrepreneur and a proven motorsport driver, Robby started his career in off-road racing, and it has remained a passion ever since.

His credentials in off-road racing are extensive, winning seven SCORE International off-road championships from 1986 to 2009, two stadium series races, and three Baja 500 and three Baja 1000 races. He participated in his first Dakar in 2005, driving for the Red Bull–sponsored Volkswagen team, and became the first US driver to win a stage in the auto category. He finished third in the first South American Dakar in 2009, and eighth in the 2010 edition.

Gordon's racing career has not been without controversy. In the March 2009 edition of the San Filpe 250 off-road race, he was accused of leaving the mandated route and driving down a cliff to bypass a difficult section of the course using the shortcut to get ahead of his competition, just as he did today on today's Dakar stage. During the 2009 Baja 500, he was stripped of his leading position when it was determined he had illegally received fuel on a highway section and also had violated local speed limits.

Well into a NASCAR race in 2005, he was involved in a spectacular crash that Gordon blamed on another driver. When the offending driver passed by on the next lap, Gordon threw his helmet at him, narrowly missing another car. Fined fifty thousand dollars for the incident, he then auctioned the helmet, raising over fifty-five thousand dollars for families that had been displaced by Hurricane Katrina in New Orleans. He has been fined for using illegal parts and adjustments to his vehicles, all honest mistakes according to Robby, failing to restart races in designated positions, and even getting into fights with other drivers.

It was, therefore, not too surprising to learn that he had been the center of attention for the Dakar organizers. You can imagine what was being said in the bivouac about a Rally organized and owned by the French, where European drivers were being challenged by a brash, in-your-face NASCAR driver from the United States in a bright-orange over-the-top huge Hummer. There was, I was sure, just a little talk about politics and nationalism being involved in the decision to disqualify Gordon, especially when French *moto* rider Cyril Despres was not being penalized for the time he spent in the mud two stages before. The extra time he took to extricate himself, with another rider's help who he allegedly then refused to assist, would have put him well out of contention for this year's title. C'est la vie, I guess.

That evening I found myself subject to a bit of the ASO imperialism when I sat at a table in the media tent apparently, as I soon learned, reserved only for ASO personnel. The tent was unusually crowded with journalists and photographers filing their stories and pictures, and I could not find a seat with a power plug I could use. One full half of a table at the back of the tent was free.

"You can't sit there," a young man with a thick, cultured French accent instructed me, wagging his finger at me. "You will have to move immediately."

"But there are no other benches available where I can plug in my computer," I told him.

"Tough, you can't sit there. These places are reserved only for ASO staff," he replied.

I tried to stare him down, but ultimately I had to squeeze myself onto another bench, muttering under my breath about the "fucking French arrogance." The journalists around me, my new friends, laughed out loud and agreed. I checked a number of times as I was working, and no one was sitting in the seats I had been asked to vacate.

Robby did not take the news of his potential disqualification lightly. He insisted the vacuum technology used in his car's ventilation system was within the ASO's rules and provided no advantage. He took us on a tour of his car, indicating the system in question and how he would be disconnecting the system for the next day's special. He also explained that his system had been inspected by the organizers during registration in Mar del Plata, and everything had passed with flying colors. To prove his point, he won the next day's special with the suspect system disconnected.

"Winning by fifteen minutes with our system unplugged just proves our point that it provided no advantage," Gordon said heatedly that following day. "I'm quite confident that we'll win our appeal and put it all behind us. From here on out, I'm going to try to win every stage, and the ASO can kiss my ass."

Robby also did not have many positive things to say about his main competition, the BMW and Mini cars racing for Team X-Raid and Mini All4 Racing. "Minis are for girls," he was quoted earlier in the Rally. Unfortunately, by the time he got to Lima, Robby may find out that it was a winners' podium full of these girly cars.

It was also interesting to see who was following the Dakar as we traveled from stage to stage. Aside from the thousands of local citizens who came out to experience what must be one of the largest spectacles ever to visit their towns and cities, there was a dedicated and large group of Rally Raid aficionados who traveled along with the caravan of *motos*, cars, and trucks for some, or all, of the Rally.

I had run into an older Turkish gentleman at many of the checkpoints and spectator areas, proudly wearing a flag and following his three *moto* privateer countrymen I met earlier in Copiapó (unfortunately down to only one after four stages!). He stayed in hotels, camped out, and even slept in his rental car, cheering his countrymen wherever he could and paying to enter the bivouac most evenings to help with their bike maintenance and to boost their spirits.

A South African gentleman I met a number of times was an engineer who worked on rally cars as a younger man, when the Dakar was still running on that continent. He was the only person I had seen who, when everyone was clustered around the driver of a car asking questions or seeking autographs, was lying on the ground, peering under the vehicle at a drive shaft or suspension system.

And then there was the very elderly Argentinian following the Dakar in his antique Ford station wagon, painted bright pink. Argentina is a haven for late-model and vintage US-manufactured automobiles, the majority in really bad shape and held together with tape, twine, and glue. It's a wonder he had made it this far.

There were also legions of motorcycles following the Dakar, some highly cognizant and careful of what they could and couldn't do, and others, like that foolishly misguided woman earlier this week, who were not. Today we entered into Arica on a two-lane highway, with one of the Dakar *moto* riders in the lane beside us. Suddenly two kids on a high-powered road bike came riding between us, slowed down to the same speed, and for a number of blocks weaved dangerously close to our truck and the competitor as his passenger tried to take pictures while standing up on the back. Another pair of morons, but at least they were wearing helmets.

On the other hand, earlier today I met with two wonderful Australian bikers on a year-long ride in aid of a local children's charity in their country. They had already been on the road for ten months, moving from north to south through Canada, the United States, and into South America, planning to follow the Dakar for a few days. Sadly mechanical issues with the hub and Ohlin shocks on their BMW motorcycles necessitated a hurried trip south to Santiago for repairs. I hoped they made it through to their eventual target destination in Ushuaia at the southern tip of the continent.

CHAPTER THIRTEEN
A MOST DISAPPOINTING DAY

With the completion of stage eleven in Arica, Chile, and given that the entire Dakar organization would once again be congregating at a border crossing the next day heading into Peru, Rodrigo and I cleared through customs in the bivouac and early in the evening headed over the border to spend the night in the town of Tacna to beat the next day's crowds at the border. This was the Dakar's first trip into Peru, and as we wandered around Tacna during a festival to welcome the Rally to the country, the people seemed a bit mystified by the event. What was all the fuss about? Yet as videos on large screens in the main town square showed highlights of the race, and bands played to the growing crowds, a sense of excitement began to take control, and we were sure the crowds would be big once the Dakar followed us into the twenty-seventh country it had visited in its thirty-four–year history.

And we were right—the roads and highways were lined with thousands of cheering spectators everywhere we went, and I had yet to see so many people at the checkpoints and spectator zones.

We checked into a decent downtown Tacna hotel and easily found local currency through a banking machine, though what the Peruvian currency is called or worth I will have to learn later. While Rodrigo went off to organize an Internet modem for the rest of the trip, I decided to sample my first true Peruvian *pisco* sour, the traditional drink of Peru and Chile.

Pisco is one of South America's most popular libations. A brandy-like liquor distilled from grapes, *pisco's* origins are widely regarded as dating from the early 1600s in Peru. The drink, first made by farmers from grapes discarded as not suitable for wine production by their

Spanish conquerors, it became popular with sailors, who called it *pisco* after the name of the port city on the southwest coast of Peru where the last Dakar bivouac of 2012 would be located. It quickly became the liquor of choice for sailors plying South America's trade routes, and by the beginning of the eighteenth century, it almost equaled wine in volume as a Peruvian export.

Unfortunately for Peru, the bulk of *pisco* production was derived from the Tarapacá region, a province that Chile annexed following their victory in the 1883 War of the Pacific. Over the next century, production of *pisco* in this new Chilean territory increased significantly to where the country now produces more than fifty times more *pisco* than Peru. To make matters worse, in the 1960s, Chile banned the import of any product from Peru that called itself *pisco*. In retaliation, Peru has tried to enforce on world markets the denomination of *pisco* as a Peruvian-only product, and has applied to internationally register the name and its country of origin with the World Intellectual Property Organization. I don't think the dispute over the origins of *pisco* will lead to another armed conflict, but if you want to inflame the rhetoric of a native from either Peru or Chile, all you need to do is comment that the other county's *pisco* is superior and then stand back.

Most first encounter the liquor in the popular *pisco* sour, a libation concocted by blending *pisco* with sugar and lemon juice. Not a day will go by when you are not offered a glass of this popular aperitif. At any restaurant meal, when you check into a hotel, visit a home, or attend an event, *pisco* sours will be served. Opinions vary as to the exact combination of these ingredients, the type of lemon or lime used, and whether or not angostura bitters should be added. Both Chileans and Peruvians take pride in their own particular recipes, and all have their favorite styles and restaurants that serve *pisco*. Our eldest son has adapted the *pisco* sour to his own taste, adding one part orange juice to the mix of lemon, resulting in another unique version of this wonderful aperitif.

But even the derivation of the *pisco* sour is disputed between Chile and Peru. The Chileans claim the drink was invented by a steward from an English ship who, setting up a bar in the northern Chilean town of Iquique, introduced a new drink, combining *pisco* with the *limon de pica*, a small lime grown in the area. Peru, however, claims that the popular drink was invented in the early 1920s at the Bar Morris in Jiron de la Union, Peru. There are quite distinct differences between Peruvian *pisco* and that produced in Chile, and debates can extend long into the night over the relative merits of each country's *pisco* sour.

Another great debate between the two countries continues over who first discovered the potato, coming to a head in 2008 during the UN's Year of the Potato. In preparing to celebrate the tuber's heritage, the UN stated that the first wild potato plants were cultivated near Lake Titicaca in southern Peru around seven thousand years ago. Chile disputed this fact, with the country's minister of agriculture boldly claiming DNA tests had shown that almost all of the seven thousand varieties of potato grown around the world are derived from plants grown on Chile's Chiloé Island. National pride in both countries became inflamed, with Peruvian editorials and the government accusing the Chileans of trying to usurp yet another national achievement, and of course bringing the War of the Pacific into the fray as a further example of the Chilean invasion of all things sacred in Peru.

Finally the scientists passed on their exhaustive studies, indicating that, in fact, both countries were correct. Their research indicated that, while it is true approximately three-quarters of potato varieties grown outside of South America are derived from Chile's native spud, it is also true that these versions were the grandchildren of Peru's original *solanum tuberosum*, a variety not found outside the country. So who won? As in all things South American, no one wins, all sides of the dispute are a little bit right, everyone claims victory, and everyone is a little bit upset.

Sitting in the Café da Vinci in Talca, Peru, I had to say that my first Peruvian *pisco* sour was pretty good. It was certainly different from the sours I had experienced in Chile, but they were all good. My only advice? Do not consume more than two *pisco* sours at any one sitting if you want to be able to walk home. They are deceptively strong.

As Rodrigo was taking some time finding his Internet modem, I broke this rule and had three big sours. It was like my first drink as a teenager. I had been living like a monk for the prior three weeks with hardly any alcohol consumption, and the three strong drinks, combined with a very early start that morning, combined to make the world a very wonderful place indeed, with everyone seemingly my best friend. I had a plate of delicious ceviche, a traditional dish of raw seafood marinated in lemon, salt, cilantro, and other spices, consumed with a local beer. Thank goodness Rodrigo came when he did and dragged me off to bed.

Day eleven of the Dakar Rally presented a few new challenges and some very sad news for the Tamarugal team. After a 171-kilometer liaison section taking the competitors over the border into Peru, the 534-kilometer special covered very challenging dirt and sand terrain, climbing numerous times from sea level through 2,000 meters on steep ascents and descents. The length of the special was mitigated by another neutralization ride through the protected areas where the famous Nazca lines are found. Adding to the challenges was the early start for the *moto* competitors, as they began departing the Arica bivouac in the dark at 4:00 a.m.

Heavy rains over the prior few days had forced the *moto* special route to be changed—the organizers were trying a new tradition to have a separate stage for the *motos* with a different bivouac from everyone else, where even the assistance vehicles could not enter. It was a tough special, with a number of the top *moto* competitors getting lost within the first forty kilometers.

Daniel, now the top Chilean rider standing overall in thirteenth position, was confident he could move up into the top ten through the final three days of the Rally. He set out in a good starting position and raced away into the dark. But his Rally was to end early in the stage as he fell over in a deep and fast-moving river, swollen by the recent rains, with the very hot engine ingesting a significant amount of water. He got the bike out of the river with help from his teammate Claudio and tried to restart the engine. Unfortunately, water had entered the cylinder head, causing the engine block to crack and the piston to break. Daniel's 2012 Rally was over. Burro, a true friend, gave him a hug and rocketed off to try to recoup the time he had spent helping him. It was a sad time for everyone on the team. Daniel was doing so well, proving he could take his place among the best in the world. We would look for big things from him next year.

Later that day more details came to light regarding Daniel's retirement. Apparently, as he approached the river, he stopped and gestured to one of the Rally's official photographers, questioning if it was safe to cross at that point. The photographer gave Daniel a thumbs-up sign and then raised his camera to shoot the crossing. When Daniel's bike fell over and submerged just shy of the opposite riverbank, a number of spectators rushed to help him, but the photographer shouted it was not allowed, threatening to record any assistance he might receive, disqualifying him. This claim, of course, was not true, and the suspicion was that the photographer dashed Daniel's 2012 Dakar dream in aid of getting a few good photos of the young Chilean struggling all alone with his bike in the water. The helpful fans brought Daniel's bike to the bivouac in their truck, and he was forced to hitchhike back. Such is the Dakar.

The drive through southern Peru was spectacular. The stark flat deserts of the high-altitude Anteplano were surrounded by sand-colored volcanos, some capped with snow. We would then drop down into lush green valleys growing vegetables, corn, and wheat, bordered by bamboo and cacti, with cows grazing, all fed by fast-moving, light-brown rivers. The region is also famed for the mysterious Nazca lines, huge drawings of mythic figures cut into the sides of mountains and on wide desert plains miles from anywhere. The image must be central to Peruvian culture, as, in most of the towns we drove through, there would be similar, more modern glyphs cut into the cliffs above. The practice even extended to advertising, with hotels, taxis, and even large multinational telecommunications companies using the tactic to promote their services. It was interesting to see and, for me, a lot more attractive than garish highway billboards.

One very large army base north of Tacna had carved its insignia and other regimental crests into the hills above, but there were *very* large and *very* clear signs in big red letters with lots of exclamation points in a number of languages telling us that no pictures or video could be taken as we passed by the base. Guard posts were strategically positioned to ensure these instructions were followed. Even this gringo did not dare raise his camera as we drove by.

Another mystery was the large number of land plots staked out in the desert and cleared for some purpose, with straight lines of stone taken from land delineating the property boundaries. Hand-lettered signs were posted telling us this land was private, and on most, a very small, perhaps five-foot- by-five-foot concrete block structure could be seen with openings for a door and window. Were these mining claims? Certainly nothing could be grown in this sand with no water. And in the miles of desert we crossed, dotted with hundreds of these plots and structures, I did not see one person. I asked a number of Peruvians what these land plots were, but no one seemed to know, or, as is so typical in South America, I received a number of dissenting opinions.

I also had a very long and much needed laugh today after hearing the disappointing news about young Daniel Gouët's retirement from the 2012 Dakar. All four of the Tamarugal Honda Ridgeline trucks had stopped at a gas station in the small town of Ormate. As in most locations, local residents were there to greet and meet the Dakar. Among the crowd was a very beautiful young woman wearing not many clothes named Pillar, who chatted pleasantly with a number of our team. Quite smitten with her, one team member (who will remain nameless but is really the son of the owner of the team), approached her with a big grin on his face.

"You have won our daily prize of a visit for you and a friend to the Tamarugal compound in the Arequipa Dakar bivouac!" he exclaimed. She accepted with great excitement. There really was no such prize, but I was sure Pillar would be treated well and receive a lot of attention this evening.

I'd be in my tent asleep, I promised.

CHAPTER FOURTEEN
THE MYSTERIOUS NAZCA LINES

Day twelve of the 2012 Dakar wrapped up in a massive dust storm just outside Nazca, Peru. In a high, flat desert area known as the San José Plains near Nazca, about 430 kilometers south of Lima, you will find numerous geoglyphs and figures known as the Nazca Lines. Utilizing radiocarbon dating, it is estimated they were constructed between 193 BC and 648 AD. The lines were made by digging furrows into the landscape between twenty centimeters and one meter deep, and lining the edges of the ditches with stones gathered from the surrounding desert. With this protection, the depth of the furrows, and the direction in which they were purposefully placed, the typically high winds in the region were somehow prevented from filling the shallow ditches with sand for some two thousand years.

The figures mostly represent humans, birds, fish, plants, and other symbols held sacred by the Nazca peoples who inhabited the region. Geometric lines and trapezoids were added to these figures over the years, and scientists, mathematicians, and archeologists have been puzzling over the reasons for decades. The lines were known to local residents as Inca Roads for many years before their "official" discovery in the early 1940s, when the true size, scale, and patterns could be seen for the first time from the air.

Many theories have been developed as to the purpose of the lines and figures. One theory proposes that the lines link the figures to aqueducts and cemeteries via "sacred paths," pointing to areas where people could gather for religious ceremonies. The zigzag geometric lines simply represent rain falling, while circles and spirals signify water flowing from springs. In such a dry desert, water was worshipped and linked to fertility.

Others believe the lines are an astronomical calendar, with the figures representing sacred celestial constellations. Supporting this theory is the fact that many of the large figures are similar to those found on Nazca pottery and textiles from the period. Another idea is that the figures and lines were simply a "make work" project to keep people busy and cope with a huge increase in the population during this time, while another proposes they are a drawing board for planned irrigation and aqueduct projects.

The most popular theory, however, is that the figures and lines were created by an alien race that visited earth centuries ago. In looking at the sheer size and odd human representation in the plains, you can understand why many would think this theory is not far off.

The figures are massive. The most controversial, an emblematic figure known as "the astronaut," is over thirty-two meters in length and easily resembles what we recognize today from science fiction movies as an alien-like figure. Some of the lines linking the figures are more than thirty kilometers long. One beautifully executed figure is believed to be a hummingbird and measures ninety-six meters long by sixty-six meters wide. A remarkable likeness of a monkey carved into the desert is 110 meters long. Another, looking like a spider, is forty-six meters in length. A highly lifelike representation of a condor, a sacred animal to most South American cultures, is 135 meters in size.

How did these so-called primitive peoples carve these figures out of the desert in such straight lines—shallow ditches that have not been filled with sand for almost two thousand years? It is a remarkable achievement and a testament to the creativity, endurance, and ultimately the artistry that supports our human experience.

Unless it really was an outer space alien culture that inscribed the lines. Time will tell, I suppose. Most importantly, however, it was an area the Dakar Rally avoided. New lines from racing *motos*, cars, and trucks would not be welcome.

The day twelve special consisted of 245 kilometers of almost all sand and dunes along Peru's Pacific coast west of the Nazca Lines protected area. The dunes surrounded the competitors in wave after wave, some rising from sea level to a height of 1,800 meters, with deep valleys where competitors easily became lost or stuck. Helicopter video footage of the day's special depicted a large number of motorcycles, quads, cars, and trucks sitting isolated, forlorn and alone in deep sand valleys, their drivers walking up the steep sand cliffs in the oppressive heat, trying to find a vantage point high enough that they could see where to go and get back on track. With few landmarks to follow and orient themselves, Rally driving with sand and dunes as far as you can see in every direction can be a nightmare. Many became stuck in these valleys and had to be rescued through the night and into the next day by the sweeper trucks and helicopters.

The sand dunes and the *polvo* in northern Chile and the first two days in Peru had taken their toll, and as we entered the final real stage where positions could change, the Dakar was down to only 192 vehicles remaining in the competition, a far cry from the 465 that began in Mar del Plata what seemed so very long ago. The Dakar has a very high attrition rate, and you can understand why just finishing this grueling challenge was a significant accomplishment.

As the Dakar wound its way toward Lima and the podium celebrations on January 15, life in the bivouac was becoming a bit more relaxed. There was more socializing, and I could see a few beers being consumed here and there as I walked past some of the team compounds, especially last night in the Tamarugal area, as, with the bikes at a separate bivouac without assistance, the mechanics had nothing else to do but get a little loaded. After a few beers, as well as shots of Jägermeister, I found that my Spanish improved immensely.

One of my traditions for motorcycle touring is to take a flask of fine single malt whisky along with me. I am a sucker for anything with the word "Glen" or "Mac" included in the brand name, and I had maintained this practice by bringing a large bottle of Macallan with me on the Dakar. As the appropriate time and place had not yet occurred to bring the whisky out, it seemed like a good time now for me to contribute to the team's rapidly diminishing sobriety.

I retrieved the flask and inquired, in my best Spanish, if anyone would like a taste of fine Scotch whisky. South Americans typically do not drink much hard liquor—wine, beer, and the inevitable *pisco* sours are their drinks of choice. Shyly, at first they all declined the offer, until Chelo, the brave soul, said he would like to try it. This broke the ice, and they all held their glasses up for me to pour a wee dram for each. But to my horror, they then proceeded to add a large glug of Red Bull to my premium single malt. Now I am not much of a snob, but this is just not done. I explained that scotch should be enjoyed neat or with a little water, and I promised to bring some bottles to the closing ceremony for all of them to enjoy properly. They promised they would behave.

Breakfast had also loosened up significantly. Through most of the Rally, the morning meal was generally quite silent, with competitors gazing seriously into the future and steeling themselves for the day's stage ahead. Now, while there was still the same intensity present, the loud dance-mix music and the synchronized moves with fingers waving in the air by the tiny Peruvian Sodexo staff lent some much needed lightness to the early mornings. However, if I never hear pop tunes remixed to the same dance beat again, it will be too soon.

The drive from Arequipa to Nazca was spectacular. The road hugged the Pacific coast, but, unlike every other ocean I had driven beside, there was no civilization in Peru to spoil the view. Beautiful unsullied beaches were bordered by steep rocky cliffs and massive fields of sand dunes. The road was in excellent condition, winding and twisting up and then down the rocky cliffs, meandering between the beach and the dunes. There was a significant amount of traffic, as this was the only north–south route for Peruvian commerce, and, combined with the Dakar train moving north, it could be very busy at times. And you hear about South American tour buses rolling off cliffs—I can understand how it happens. There is little protection with few guardrails, and truckers simply take for granted that you will slow down or stop if they pass and accelerate directly toward you. It's a bit scary, but the views are like nothing I have ever seen. It would be a perfect road to tour by motorcycle.

And the Peruvians continued to turn out in the thousands to welcome the Dakar, waving flags, clapping, cheering, and asking for photos. One sign in English said it all: "You Dakar guys are crasy [sic]!"

Tonight was my last in a Dakar bivouac. My wonderful and beautiful wife was flying from Canada to Lima tomorrow, and I was going to miss the final bivouac near the town of Pisco to drive straight through to

Lima to meet her. I managed to bribe Rodrigo with the promise of a first-class hotel room and an expensive dinner if he would detour from the Pisco bivouac and drive with me to Lima. He did not need much encouragement. I would miss the sense of community in the Dakar world, but I had to admit I wouldn't miss my tent.

My shelter for the past few weeks was quite a feat of engineering. Wrapped in a round bag about twenty-four inches in diameter and maybe an inch thick, the device sprung automatically open into a fully formed one-person tent once it was removed from its protective bag. All that was great, except you had to get it back into the bag the next morning, and after two weeks, I still could not figure out how to fold it properly. I am not very mechanically inclined, but being defeated by a tent was particularly embarrassing, especially when I had to drag it sheepishly over to the same Tamarugal guy every morning to ask him to put it away for me. He did it in about three seconds, looking at me with increasing disdain and, I was sure, shaking his head about *"el stupido gringo."* Despite watching intently, I still couldn't do it. Maybe next year.

CHAPTER FIFTEEN
THE 2012 DAKAR ENDS

This morning in the Nazca bivouac, an absolute miracle happened as I made up for being significantly tent challenged through the almost two weeks I had spent on the Dakar. The first night my designated tent was broken, and I had to sleep in the bed of our truck. And once I was provided with a replacement, I could set it up easily, but for the life of me, like Humpty Dumpty, I could not put it back together again. Until this morning. Somehow, after fourteen embarrassing trips to have one of my team members fold it for me, I somehow managed to get it in the bag all by myself. A bit like riding a bicycle—once you do it successfully, you know how to do it forever. But it took until my last night in a bivouac.

And what a night it was. All through the afternoon, high winds whipped up the sands of the Peruvian desert around Nazca, and, combined with the thousands of spectators driving to and fro and stirring up even more dust, it was the worst night of *polvo* I had encountered on the Dakar. It got into everything—your eyes, your hair, your mouth, your clothing. Everyone was covered by a thin gray coating, requiring a lot of water to get clean. And there was not a lot of water in the desert.

The 2012 Dakar Rally essentially finished today with stage thirteen from Nazca to Pisco, a tough 275 kilometers of track and sand dunes ending at the bivouac in Pisco. Like the day before, the special covered huge areas of untracked sand and dunes where navigation could make or break the chance of finishing the 2012 Dakar. The valleys between the massive dunes all could look the same, and it was so easy to become lost. Organizers also cautioned riders in the briefing meeting the night before to be very aware of the lack of sleep and rest they had endured since the rest days in Copiapó. On the last real race special, competitors needed to pace themselves to be sure they made it through.

Tomorrow was the drive to the podium finish in Lima, with only a short twenty-six–kilometer special in the middle designed to show the Lima fans what the Dakar was all about. It was possible that the *moto* category may need this short stage to determine a winner, as, after today, Marc Como led Cyril Despres by the scant margin of just over a minute.

But it all became a bit anticlimactic during stage thirteen, as Como suffered engine trouble and Despres was declared the winner of the 2012 Dakar *moto* category.

I spent the last night of my Dakar adventure in Lima sitting in the bar of the Marriott Hotel overlooking the Pacific Ocean, watching some surfers catch waves, and enjoying some delicious fresh salmon ceviche and wine with my wife and Rodrigo. The contrast with the past two weeks could not be starker, but also welcome, I had to admit. A hot, and blessedly private, shower, real soap and shampoo, clean towels, a functioning toilet, a big bed with sheets, real grown-up laundered clothes—these were luxuries I had not experienced for some time. Yet as I walked around Lima with Karen, I was also a bit sad this adventure was coming to an end. There was a lot I would miss about the Dakar, the bivouacs, and the excitement of seeing finely tuned *motos*, cars, and trucks master the desert, supported by highly dedicated crews working hard for the glory of conquering the Dakar. As one car driver told me, "the Dakar is only designed to wreck our vehicles and test our skill and patience as drivers and navigators." It was a true triumph to simply finish the Dakar, and kudos to everyone who achieved this goal.

As promised, tonight we were treating Rodrigo to a well-deserved dinner in a highly recommended restaurant, one that specialized in preparing the local delicacy of guinea pig, to thank him for everything he did for me. He was a wonderful companion, a translator, a communicator of stories and gossip he picked up in the bivouacs and on the stages, and somehow he kept his patience with this stupid gringo along for the ride. I was very appreciative, and if anyone is looking for a terrific sports photographer and a great guy, I can highly recommend Rodrigo Farias.

The 2012 Dakar Rally culminated in the traditional closing podium ceremony in the *Plaza des Armas*, a huge public square in the center of

Lima, Peru. Our hotel was quite some distance from the square, and we departed early to make sure we arrived in time for Rodrigo to take photos of the team. Everyone had worked so hard to get here, and it was important for him to capture the emotions of a job well done.

But it was a close call. We thought the truck's Tripy system would guide us to the location, and it did indicate with an arrow which direction we should drive, but as we navigated away from the hotel, the arrow kept swinging around and the distance to the destination was increasing instead of reducing. Rodrigo, unlike most men, believes in asking for help frequently, as in South America everyone seems to know a better way to get somewhere, and the advice can be quite contradictory. After a few residents told us to simply drive *frente, frente, frente*, meaning "straight ahead," we stopped to ask three police officers standing near a popular beachfront. It turned out we were very lost, heading in the wrong direction, and the complicated directions to get to the right road occupied about five minutes of valuable time. Finally, one officer shouted to his partner on a motorcycle, two others stopped the busy highway traffic, and the bike headed out in front of us with lights flashing to guide us up and around a circuitous route to a rather large eight-lane highway heading back into town.

The highway was crowded with cars heading toward the Dakar ceremony, and everyone smiled and waved as we drove along. We then encountered a line of police closing off the highway and diverting traffic up a ramp onto the busy city streets. But when they saw our truck with the Dakar registrations, they opened up the gates and we found ourselves driving down an eight-lane expressway all by ourselves.

Well, not exactly by ourselves. The bulk of the Dakar convoy had driven along this route earlier in the day, having departed the Pisco bivouac at four thirty in the morning. So we were all alone on the multilane highway, surrounded on both sides and on every bridge overpass for at least five or six kilometers by people lining five deep, cheering, waving, clapping, flying flags and signs—thousands and thousands of Peruvians enthusiastically welcoming two gringos and a Chilean to their city. My wife, who I don't think had really understood how big the Dakar is, was astonished. It was quite a spectacle.

We arrived into the downtown core, and the Tripy started to make some sense, telling us we were very close and to head off a roundabout in a specific direction. But everywhere we went, the roads were closed and thronged with thousands of people milling about, paying no heed to a large Dakar truck trying to get through. We tried following other Dakar vehicles, but they were as lost as we were. The problem was we did not want to drive to the square where the closing ceremonies were being held, as the Tripy wanted, but rather to a closed area about twenty blocks from the *Plaza des Armas,* where all the Dakar vehicles were securely parked at a Peruvian army base. And as we were trying to drive in one direction, everyone else was heading in the opposite. It was getting tense.

As Rodrigo said later, "the Dakar and Tamarugal must have good karma," because somehow we found ourselves finally where we wanted to be, with a bus holding the rest of the team waiting for us. We quickly parked the truck, jumped on the bus, and away we went through the throngs of crowds to the central square.

What a scene greeted us. Escorted by police and huge guys in blue T-shirts with "Bouncer" written on them, we were rushed through various security checkpoints onto a patio behind the main podium. Here, every participant who finished the Dakar was introduced to a crowd estimated at over 120,000 people. We could see the two Prohens brothers and Burro in line to go up, and we waited for a few minutes, along with a disappointed but excited Daniel Gouët, who had stayed with his team since he was forced to retire with engine failure three days before. When Daniel's three teammates climbed the ramp to the podium, we were all escorted out onto the platform to accompany them, where, with deafening crowd noise and racing engines under a rain of golden-colored streamers, champagne was uncorked and sprayed around and hugs were exchanged. Despite my insignificant role in the success of the Tamarugal team, I was incredibly moved and tears filled my eyes. What a trip it had been.

After watching a few other teams celebrate, we headed back to the bus, crawled through dense crowds back to the vehicle compound, and then jumped in our trucks to go to the team hotel. Karen and I grabbed a cab and returned to our hotel on the beachfront. Before leaving, Karen presented Rodrigo and the team with two huge bottles of Macallan single malt whisky, as promised a few nights earlier. The group assured me that no Red Bull would be added to their drinks. As we said our good-byes for the evening, there were all sorts of plans to attend the huge Dakar closing party in a downtown stadium, meet for dinner or drinks, but truly everyone was so exhausted and, with the adrenaline depleted, no one had any energy left. It was time for sleep. We would all catch up some time later in Santiago. My Dakar adventure was over.

So how did everyone I met do on this year's Dakar? As we know, Daniel retired on stage eleven in thirteenth position following his unfortunate battle in the river, a real accomplishment and proof he can compete with the best. Felipe Prohens finished in twenty-eighth position, moving up from his starting position at forty-one, while his brother Jaime was close behind in thirty-second place. Burro was right behind him in thirty-third position. Everyone on the Tamarugal team had moved up in the rankings, positioning them strongly to compete in next year's Dakar.

Camélia Liparoti, the Italian quad rider I met earlier in the Rally, achieved her dream of finishing in the top ten by completing her Dakar in ninth place. Unfortunately, none of the Turkish *moto* privateers were able to complete their Dakar, but I was sure they would be back next year with the valued experience gained on their Dakar helping them to improve. Captain Rally also failed to finish, but he did gain a lot of positive media coverage for the Chilean military, his prime goal.

As was forecast early in the Rally, the new Minis were all but unchallenged in the car category, finishing first, second, and fourth, with a Toyota in third position. There were five Minis completing the 2012 Dakar in the top ten.

The truck category was once again dominated by the Dutch de Rooy family, who took both first and second place in this highly competitive group. A team from Kazakhstan finished third, almost two hours behind the two top Dutch teams.

My Canadian compatriot David Bensadoun kept improving through the Rally and completed his first Dakar in thirty-ninth place, a real success story. I was sure he believed he could do even better next year. Robby Gordon, despite his protestations, saw his disqualification hold up and did not place on the podium. He also probably had to eat a little bitter crow as he watched the so-called "girly" Minis take first, second, fourth, and seventh place in the overall standings. Neither of the Hummers was able to complete the 2012 Dakar.

CHAPTER SIXTEEN
WHAT DOES THE DAKAR MEAN?

As we drove through a small town in Peru near the end of the Rally, a man on a bicycle approached our truck and asked Rodrigo, "What does Dakar mean?"

Perplexed, Rodrigo looked at me to help with an answer. "You're the writer. What does this all mean?" he questioned. I simply shrugged my shoulders. It was one of those questions that required a lot of thought and time. Or it could be answered quite simply. After staring at me for a minute or two, and the poor Peruvian fan becoming more perplexed as the silence wore on, Rodrigo took the simple approach.

"It's a city in West Africa where the Rally used to finish," he answered lamely. The man left, puzzled by our response.

But what does the Dakar mean, and why do people embark on these two-plus weeks of madness? The dangers are widely recognized—everyone knows how many people have been killed or seriously injured over the Rally's relatively short history. They are well aware of the threats to their general health, including disease, dehydration, altitude sickness, heat stroke, and numerous other problems that are encountered each and every day during a Dakar Rally.

And why do people engage in high-risk activities at all? What drives people to leave the comforts of home and family to challenge themselves with a potential, and in some cases highly likely, nasty ending?

Given the cost to society of high-risk endeavors, for decades psychologists have been studying the drive to participate in such activities as Rally racing, mountain and rock climbing, backcountry skiing, and other sports where the threat to life and limb is ever present. Mountain climbing is now among North America's fastest-growing sports, and extreme skiing, where you descend sheer cliffs of loose snow, easily avalanche-able, and then launch yourself from rocky ledge to ledge, is gaining wider popularity. Paragliding, parachuting, and bungee jumping are now de facto normal and unchallenged activities for corporate retreats and team-building exercises. Adventure holidays, offering such high-risk activities as white-water rafting and dangerous wildlife safaris, have grown to become a multimillion-dollar tourism business.

Consider the fact that backcountry skiing kills more people per capita than any other high-risk sport, and more likely than not you will die slowly, freezing and suffocating to death upside down in the dark after falling and wedging yourself into a deep ice crevasse. It is the stuff of nightmares. Yet many of my best friends head out every year into the mountains on their backcountry skis, and they are among the sanest, most well-adjusted people I know, all with families and intellectually rewarding careers. It is most perplexing.

A study by researchers at Vanderbilt University and the Albert Einstein College of Medicine suggests a biological explanation for why certain people hurl themselves, some would say recklessly, into these life-threatening activities. The reason, the study postulates, lies in the amount of the neurochemical dopamine in our systems.[1]

Dopamine is the brain's "feel-good" chemical. It is responsible for normal people feeling satisfied after a good meal, when our favorite sports team wins a game, when we receive praise for a job well done, and even when we react positively to drug use, such as cocaine, marijuana, and alcohol. It is also what makes us get a high when we successfully ski a black diamond mountain run, win at the blackjack table, or daringly exceed the speed limit when driving on a beautiful and scenic country road.

---

1   The theories and ideas about why people engage in high-risk activities are taken from a number of articles and journals, including *Psychology Today* ("Risk" by Paul Roberts, published on November 1, 1994, and updated on June 17, 2010), *Time* ("Why we Take Risks—It's the Dopamine" by Alice Parks, published on December 30, 2008), the University of Nevada at Las Vegas *Lee Business School Research Digest* ("What Were They Thinking? Examining Choices Over Risky Recreation" by Mary Riddel) and the *SummitPost* ("Living on the Edge: Extreme Sports and their Role in Society" posted by "mountaingirlBC" on August 9, 2010).

Risk takers' brains, the researchers believe, are more saturated with dopamine, predisposing them to engage in ever more dangerous endeavors, and because they get such a big hit of dopamine when the risk is high, they keep coming back for more. In addition, it is possible that the risk taker's brain, according to a report in the *Journal of Neuroscience*, contains fewer dopamine-inhibiting receptors, those other chemicals in our bodies that monitor the levels of dopamine we are receiving and signal the brain to stop producing it when the level is sufficient.

Research has shown that the enzyme monoamine oxidase (MAO) plays an important role in regulating levels of arousal, inhibition, and excitement. The MAO enzyme regulates the levels of such important neurotransmitters as norepinephrine, which awakens the brain to stimuli, the feel-good chemical dopamine, and serotonin, which acts as a brake on norepinephrine and inhibits arousal. People who seek ever-riskier sensations may have lower base levels of norepinephrine and can tolerate more stimulation before serotonin kicks in to say enough is enough.

Take as another example Seattle, Washington–based lawyer Jim Wickwire. This father of five and successful attorney is best known for being the first American to climb Pakistan's K2, the second highest mountain in the world and reputably the sport's most challenging ascent. On the climb he lost a number of his toes to frostbite and half a lung to altitude sickness. On a previous climb he watched two friends fall to their deaths, while on another mountain trip he helplessly saw another companion freeze to death after becoming wedged in a crevasse. (I told you this happens!) He then tried to climb Mount Everest, the world's highest mountain, turning back after another partner died in the attempt. A few years later, at the ripe old age of fifty-three, he was preparing for a second attempt at ascending Everest. And everyone knows how many people die trying to conquer this mountain every year.

"I have stopped asking why I climb," Wickwire admits. "People who engage in this activity are probably driven to it in a psychological fashion that they may not even understand themselves."

This predisposition among the risk-taking part of our society may seem problematic, but it may also contribute to a richer, more diverse universe in which we live and, more importantly, can inform us as to why, as a species, we are here at all.

Svante Paabo[2] heads the Department of Evolutionary Genetics at the Max Planck Institute of Evolutionary Anthropology in Leipzig, Germany. For a number of years he has been working on a massive project to sequence the genome of Neanderthal, a species of "not quite" humans that disappeared from our planet eons ago. Neanderthals were a parallel species that competed for survival with Homo sapiens, our ancestors, and were apparently bigger, stronger, tougher, and perhaps even more intelligent—fossils indicate they had a bigger head than those of our direct ancestors.

Yet, despite being established more than two hundred thousand years before Homo sapiens appeared, it is believed Neanderthal became extinct. Studies have shown that as they spread out from their origins in Europe and Western Asia, they stopped whenever they reached a natural obstacle like open water or high mountain ranges. In Paabo's view, this is one of the basic differences between us, Homo sapiens, and Neanderthal, and why we survived—we kept going. He believes there is some element in our DNA that drives us to take calculated risk. It's why we first ventured out on water where you cannot see land, it's why we crossed massive mountain ranges to see what's on the other side, it's why we went to the moon, and it's maybe why crazy people enter the Dakar Rally.

"There is, I like to think, some madness there. How many people must have sailed out and vanished in the Pacific Ocean before finding Easter Island? It's ridiculous. And why do you do that? Is it for glory? For immortality? For curiosity? And now we try to go to Mars—it never stops," Paabo exclaimed.

"If we one day know that some freak mutation made the human insanity and exploration thing possible, it will be amazing to think that it was this little inversion on this chromosome that made all this happen

---

2 Svante Paabo's theories, and my interpretations about his ideas on the differences between Neanderthal and Homo sapiens, were taken from Elizabeth Colbert's fascinating article "Sleeping with the Enemy" published in *The New Yorker* magazine on August 15, 2011.

and changed the whole ecosystem of the planet and made us dominate everything. We are all crazy in some way—what drives this?" he asked.

The brain's "feel-good" chemical dopamine may also contribute another factor, as it is linked to "approach behaviors," such as feeding, fighting, foraging, and exploration. The willingness to take risks, even if only by a few members of a group, could result in huge and lasting benefits. Moving into a new area, ancient Homo sapiens would have to quickly assess their safety—which water was okay to drink, which cave was empty, or did it contain a huge, dangerous, carnivorous, and hungry dinosaur? Someone, predisposed to take the risk, would have to test the water by drinking it first and also be the first to enter the cave to see if anything was there. This ability to enter the unknown, accept the risk, and even sacrifice their life is perhaps another reason Homo sapiens endured and why we are here today.

Increased levels of dopamine and the possible imbalance of other neurochemicals are an important part of the story, but there may be other societal factors in the world today that drive people to take risk. For example, upbringing, personal experience, socioeconomic status, and education may all combine to determine how the impulse to take risk is ultimately expressed. While they may have entered motorcycle racing at an early age, Dakar *moto* competitors are part of a tight-knit community with its own language, knowledge base, standards of excellence, and culture. The "learned aspect" is an important element in a risk taker's lifestyle—the intellectual or conscious side of deciding to participate in a Dakar. Working through a challenge can itself be a powerful motivator. As David Bensadoun told me, one of the attractions of participating in a Dakar was the chance to solve problems, to anticipate everything that could possibly happen, and to try to prepare for their occurrence.

Finally, with our ever-more governed society, one in which we are increasingly legislated from taking risks, traditional outlets to appease the attraction to any level of danger are fast disappearing. As civilization minimizes natural risks—try to find a true wilderness experience anywhere in the world today—and stability is enforced through repressive laws and social mores, those among us with a propensity to encounter risky activities are being forced to look further afield to appease their drive.

But for most of us, risk taking is also a means to cope with the boredom of our lives and to manage the anxieties that plague everyday existence. Risk taking, no matter what level we push ourselves to, can lead to a sense of self-esteem and confidence, and possibly result in more societal benefits than otherwise might be thought.

Successful entrepreneurs assess and then take risks in starting their businesses. People who enter political life, assuming they have altruistic goals, are taking a risk in leaving behind their former careers and lives to run for election for the benefit of us all. Taking an unpopular stand on issues, while often for the right reason and leading to important societal reform, can be a very high-risk proposition. Think about Martin Luther King and Lech Walesa, or even the little, unknown guy who stood in front of the tank in Tiananmen Square during the suppression of the student uprising in China. Explorers who entered unknown landscape in search of the earth's poles, dangerous regions of the African continent, or the source of the Amazon, or scientists seeking to cure disease—all of these risky stands led, or may ultimately lead, to improve the societies in which we live. Even the high-risk decision to emigrate—leaving one life behind to risk another new one—is responsible for the settling and success of countries like Canada, Australia, and even the powerful United States of America.

And on a more basic note, taking a risk, pushing against the boundaries and strictures that govern our everyday lives, can help define who we are. As Bensadoun told me, "one of the reasons I love the world of Rally raid is that it takes me away from the boredom of my everyday life."

The noted neurologist Oliver Sacks, in his new book "Hallucinations," posits that "to live on a day-to-day basis is insufficient for human beings; we need to transcend, transport, escape; we need meaning, understanding and explanation; we need to see over-all patterns in our lives. And we need freedom (or at least the illusion of freedom) to get beyond ourselves, whether with telescopes and microscopes and our ever-burgeoning technology or in states of mind that allow us to travel to other worlds, to rise above our immediate surroundings."[3] Sacks' book

---

3 Oliver Sacks, "Altered States—Self-Experiments in Chemistry," published in *The New Yorker* magazine, August 27, 2012.

describes how people use hallucinogenic and other mind-altering drugs, and their ability to directly stimulate many complex brain functions, as a shortcut to this transcendence of ordinary life. High-risk activities, for many people, can provide the same high and transcendental moments.

Perhaps we all don't need the life-threatening experience of a Dakar Rally to help us endure and understand our place, who we really are, but all of us look for some outlet that says, "I am special."

In my case, riding motorcycles is an important method of alleviating the dullness of everyday existence and the worries about meeting the mortgage, having enough money to retire, whether our children are okay, and who will win American Idol. Aside from life with my wife, who is the most exciting person I know and who constantly challenges me, heading out on a powerful, well-engineered two-wheeled motorcycle is a thrill I have enjoyed since I was a young man. What is it about this strange vehicle that attracts me? Motorcycles can be highly dangerous—as we say, every accident is our fault, as seldom do we escape unscathed. They are not very efficient as a means of transportation, and inclement weather renders them essentially useless.

Certainly I have every reason not to like these dangerous vehicles. My father lost his arm in a motorcycle accident during the second World War.

As a child, I was not that curious as to what had happened to cause this loss. My dad could do everything all the other dads could do: he played a good game of golf; he drove to work and home every day in what were some very cool cars with standard transmissions; he swam in our pool with no inhibitions about the stump on his left shoulder; he danced gracefully with my mother to the music of Sinatra and Ella; he barbecued steaks; and he mixed a very mean martini, which he would tuck into his breast pocket when he danced. For most of my childhood, I thought dads with two arms looked kind of strange.

It was not until I was in my forties that I found out what had happened to his arm. He did not like to talk about the accident, and it took a journalist interviewing him for a story on a radical new surgery he had undergone, curing his phantom pain, to reveal the events. Dad had been a flight instructor for the Fleet Air Arm during the Second World War, the air force attached to the British Royal Navy that flew from aircraft carriers. He taught his young protégés on dry land in the South of England, commuting to and from his barracks on a BSA motorcycle he had acquired.

One of the flying skills they were taught was to make a "forced landing," to get the plane down safely without any engine power. In October 1945, my father was practicing this skill over the Zeals airfield in Southern England, flying at about one thousand feet and then cutting the engine and working to get the correct glide speed while at the same time looking for a safe place to land. He was supposed to power up the engine when he was about 250 feet off the ground, circle around, and try again. But as he put on full power on this practice run, he heard a *pop* and the engine caught on fire. With flames spilling out of the cowling, he cut the engine, pulled the fire extinguishing foam lever, and glided in for a real forced landing.

As he told me, it was a "lousy landing"—he came in far too high and far too fast, hitting the ground hard, bending the prop, and collapsing the landing gear as he careened off the runway. He was put in an ambulance and sent to a field hospital, where, after some tests, he was pronounced fine and able to return to his barracks.

But he was not okay, and on the motorcycle ride back to his barracks, he blacked out and came off his bike, hitting a tree and badly breaking his arm. His only memory of the accident was regaining consciousness briefly and hearing a rescuer say he was going to pull the spark plug cap off the racing engine. The handlebar had apparently punctured the gas tank, and fuel was leaking onto the hot and still running engine. Dad apparently shouted, "For God's sake no! Use the valve lifter to stop the engine or you will kill us all." If the cap had been lifted, the still sparking plug would have ignited the leaking fuel and gas fumes, causing a massive explosion. It was a close call.

It was not until he was sent home to Canada in December 1945 that his arm was amputated by a qualified doctor. And he was only nineteen years old.

My first real exposure to motorcycles, and the beginning of my lifelong fascination with them, arose from watching the opening scenes of David Lean's 1962 epic film *Lawrence of Arabia*, in which Peter O'Toole undertakes a ten-minute ritual to start his Brough Superior motorcycle. The camera then perches on his shoulder as O'Toole rides down picturesque English country lanes, unfortunately to his death. I was also drawn into the motorcycle culture by the 1968 Lindsay Anderson film *If*. While the movie provided my first glimpse of a naked woman engaged in carnal pursuits, my most enduring memory of the film was Malcolm McDowell's ride through the English countryside on a stolen Triumph motorcycle.

I remember mentioning these movie influences to my father, knowing he had owned a similar bike in similar surroundings. He told me with one arm he could never ride again, but if he had not lost his arm, he would certainly still own motorcycles.

My dad could not ride a motorcycle anymore. But I could, and I have been riding since I was nineteen.

Many say riding a bike gives them a sense of freedom—the wind in their hair, full sensory awareness of their environment, being alone in the world. While there may be some truth to this description, for me it does not capture the essence of motorcycling. Riding a motorcycle encompasses a number of concepts that I believe transform it into one of the more unique experiences life can offer—ritual, focus, community, and image, all of which lead to a very special intrinsic joy.

Ritual is very important in riding a motorcycle. It starts with a pre-ride inspection. Before heading out, we check tire pressures, brakes, lights, and oil levels. Any leaks must be dealt with, except, of course, for old British motorcycles, when a lack of leaks spells trouble. Ritual extends into riding habits—where to place yourself in a lane, how to look around corners, where to place your weight, how to ride in a group, ensuring you can be seen, and wearing the right clothing. All of these rituals keep a rider safe, but they are also an important element of the experience of riding.

Focus is another unique aspect of riding. Unlike other modes of transportation where distractions are an important part of the technology—sound systems, navigation systems, video systems, and communication systems—on a motorcycle these distractions can kill you. Riding demands full concentration, a full focus on the bike, the road, and the environment around you. If you find your mind wandering, you know it's time to pull over for a break. You don't listen to music or talk on the phone, and any navigation system designed for motorcycles is simple and easy to see with a quick glance. Riding must be a highly focused activity, and one of its joys is that it forces you to push away the trials and tribulations of the rest of your life. You truly are one with the motorcycle, and that is all that matters.

There is a sense of community when owning and riding a motorcycle. I like to say that I can enter a bar and, where normally someone might want to punch my lights out (I can be very irritating at times), if he owns a bike, we can always find common ground to talk. When you pass another bike on the road, most give a quick hand wave, an acknowledgment of like-minded individuals. There are certain restaurants on certain days where you can always find a group of riders to share a meal, experiences, and possibly a ride together. Motorcycling cuts across all lines of gender, race, economic standing, religion, and origin. It is a true leveler.

Despite what a rider will tell you, image is important. There is a sense of the outlaw, the individual, in becoming a motorcycle enthusiast. Wearing leather clothing and climbing off a cool bike attract a lot of attention no matter where you are. It is strangely satisfying to see the wistful glances of a wife, knowing she is thinking, *I wish I could get on the back with him*, while the husband, usually looking a little pissed, is simply thinking, *I wish I were him*. Image is the least important aspect to riding, but it is certainly there.

Ultimately, all of these elements lead to indefinable moments of intrinsic joy. You are not sure why, you are not sure where the emotion comes from, but you can be riding on a sunny day, alone on a twisty road surrounded by beautiful scenery, and you simply break out in a big grin. That, for me, is what it is about motorcycling. But none of this matters in the Dakar.

So what did the Dakar mean to me? It was an ordeal, with weeks of early pre-dawn starts and long days, little sleep, and no comfort. It was dirty, oh so dirty, living in dust and wind mostly in a desert environment. It was driving, traveling almost ten thousand kilometers in two weeks. It was noisy, as everything you did was to the sound of loud race-tuned engines, generators humming, tools, and mechanics working. It was an adventure, visiting three different South American countries, experiencing cultural aspects, and seeing sights that no tour group would ever find. It was dangerous, with the Rally experiencing one tragic death and a number of serious injuries. It was exciting, watching the *motos*, cars, and trucks compete to win, or simply to finish. It was a community, with people from all over the world gathering together in the bivouac, sharing meals, stories, and different cultural backgrounds. But most of all, the Dakar was companionship, getting to know a team of professionals and great people who worked so well together, were so good to me, and who will be friends for life.

That is what the Dakar means to me, and I will never forget this marvelous adventure.

Except I will try to forget about the tent.

ACKNOWLEDGMENTS

There are many, many people who contributed to my Dakar adventure in so many ways and helped me realize my dream to experience the excitement, drama, and companionship of the Dakar for the three weeks I traveled with the Tamarugal Honda Chile team.

I extend my sincere appreciation to Omar Campillay, the main sponsor of the team and the owner of Transportes Tamarugal Ltda, and his son Javier Campillay, the team's top car driver and a true character, for allowing me to become a member of the team.

The entire Gouet family—Pedro, his wife Soledad, and their daughters, relatives, and friends welcomed me, helped me, and, despite my faltering Spanish, made me feel like a true member of their extended family.

Their son, *moto* rider Daniel Gouet, along with his mechanic/partner Chelo, were an inspiration to me throughout the Dakar, demonstrating time and time again that this Rally was much more than just a race.

Indeed, everyone on the Tamarugal team went out of their way to help, teach, and take care of me, despite the problems with my damn tent, and I thank everyone for making me feel a part of the adventure.

Rodrigo Farias, the team's photographer and publicist, was a great companion during the long days in our truck, and his assistance and translating were invaluable each and every day.

My talented daughter, Sarah Keenlyside, forced me to enter the world of social media, and I thank her for the resulting introductions to a world of Dakar fans spanning the globe.

Finally, without the support of my beautiful wife, Karen, who lets me go on these adventures, I send my love and thanks for indulging me.